Hey FionA

LEGACIDE

WHY LEGACY THINKING IS THE SILENT KILLER OF INNOVATION

SLAY Legacy

Richard Mulholland

TMP TRACEY McDONALD PUBLISHERS

First published by Cultovation, 2014
This edition published by Tracey McDonald Publishers, 2017
Suite No. 53, Private Bag X903, Bryanston, South Africa, 2021
www.traceymcdonaldpublishers.com

ISBN 978-0-620-72726-6

Layout and design by Scala Designs (www.scaladesigns.co.za)
Illustrations by Wonderland Collective (www.wonderlandcollective.co.za)
Cover design by Firing Squad (www.firingsquad.co.za)
Printed and bound by Creda Communications

CONTENTS

FOREWORD

A foreword? Really? In a book about legacy?

Traditionally *(that's a word you're going to learn to hate)*, forewords were written by someone famous to add to the credibility and to stroke the ego of the primary author - which puts me in a little bit of a pickle... I'm not famous *(not in this timeline, anyway)*, and the idea of stroking Richard's ego makes me want to take a chemical shower.

So, let me try and add some value by prefacing the man honestly, as well as the content of his first book. I'll keep it brief.

Business, when you think about it, is a bit of a strange cat. We're all constantly trying to build *upward*, but we're always building *on* something else - 'what we did yesterday'. At the rate at which ideas, best-practice and processes are becoming obsolete *(faster than Apple's operating systems)*, the foundations upon which we build are often pockmarked with stupid, with illogic and with nonsense - and that isn't bothering people *nearly* enough...

To quote Messrs Chapman, Gilliam, Cleese, Idle and Palin, "Lad, I built this kingdom up from nothing. When I started here, all there was was swamp. Other kings said I was daft to build a castle on a swamp, but I built it all the same, just to show 'em. It sank into the swamp."

And these are, indeed, swampy times... There's daft everywhere, and yet we keep building.

Richard has never been one for just accepting things the way they are. His mission, for the 14-odd years I've known him, has been to fight against the stupid. For god's sake, he has **'Question Everything'** tattooed on his arm. And he's always doing it with an eye to make things *better*, not just *different (the two are often mutually exclusive)*. And that's why he's the perfect person to make you question your own 'everything'.

But really it's the *how* he does it that draws people to him like a smart gravity-well. Contrary to popular corporate belief, rudeness, a lack of tact, volume, insults and language that would make Eddie Murphy glance uncomfortably around the room, are not barriers, but *chisels.* Little, angry tartan chisels that slowly gouge away at years of inessential, fallacy and ordinary, until all you're left with is the truth. Like it, or not.

I've borne witness to this in every meeting we've been in together. If you've ever been in one of those meetings *(in which he may, or may not, have been wearing pants)* you know what I'm talking about. And, if you've ever seen him speak live, you definitely do, too.

For the rest of you - you're about to find out.

So, now that I've overshot brevity and passed right through into verbosity, it's time for me to shut it, and for you to watch your assumptions as they're slowly chipped away.

Me? I'm off to find that chemical shower.

D'ave Meyer
Missing Link

LEGACIDE

LEGACY: WHY LEGACY IS THE SILENT KILLER OF INNOVATION

"Some look at things that are and ask why. I dream of things that never were, and ask why not."
- George Bernard Shaw

For years this has been the prevailing wisdom for change, forward thinking and innovation - to look at things that don't yet exist and ask "why not?" What could be new? What would be different? What has never been done before?

This book is not about any of those. Not at all. In fact, it's quite the opposite. I want you to ask, "Why did we do this in the first place?" a whole lot more.

You need to understand that innovation is not limited to doing something new. In fact, more often than not, innovation should be about stopping doing something that's old - even if that thing you stop is what made you successful in the first place.

Because those very things - the stupid, inane things that would shrivel in the light of logic given half the chance - are **Legacide.** The things that are inherited or accepted as law. The things we don't question. The things that are slowing you down, and holding you back.

And that's the purpose of this book, to get you to question everything.

Don't get me wrong, I'm not suggesting that you shouldn't be shooting for the stars with all your fancy new ideas, I just think that there's a lot of cool stuff to be doing on the ground, too. Y'know - before you go.

For example, here's a few 'on the ground' questions you should be asking yourself:

- Why do 90% of my meetings get scheduled for an hour?
- Why does my receptionist answer the phone?
- Why do I believe that my kids must attend a good university?

Some of these are clearly more important that others, but they're all interesting questions. You see I'm not hoping to change the world here. I'm simply hoping to change the way that you look at it, and maybe some of the silly, unnecessary Legacidey things you accept as 'normal'. Ok - and I'll take the world, too.

Legacide is the virus that's killing off innovation in your business, and it exists in the brain of every person that has ever seen one of their ideas or projects achieve a level of success. It's legacy, it's history, it's the stuff we 'know for sure', and it's the stuff that is at the very essence of the business - and a cancer at the heart of it. Legacide is a ruthless bitch, it attaches itself to the minds of key people and it doesn't let go. To let go of a legacy would be as hard as getting my children's' mum to admit that my kids are not the most beautiful in the world *(of course if she did, she'd be lying - my children are, in fact, better looking than yours).*

Let's kick this into gear, shall we?

You know what arrived at my doorstep the other day? **The phone book!** Way back when, if we needed to find someone's number, the easiest *(and only)* way was to check the phone book - it made perfect sense then. However, fast forward a few years and we could phone directory enquiries *(the book became slightly less useful)*. Fast forward even further and we can Google them (the book is only used in strong man competitions *riiiiiip*, and yet it's still delivered). Pretty stupid when you think about it, right? That, my friends, is **Legacide!**

Another example of would be today's music industry. If I asked you to look at your CD collection and pick one at random, then asked you how many songs were on it, you would probably tell me that there were around twelve. If I then asked you to tell me how many of those songs are amazing, alright, and crap in that order, it's a safe bet that your answer would be around three, four, and five. I know this because I ask this question to audiences in conferences, brainstorms and workshops all the time and always get the same answers.

This leaves me wondering why anyone would bother to record the five duds?

So why do they? Artists in the 1950s would have had to record the full twelve, as that's how many songs would fit on an LP - a disk that was based on, for the most part, a gramophone record *(which was in turn a technology originally designed for lab use, and not music).* Those disks were expensive to record and even more expensive to distribute - so maximising what you put on it was crucial.

Fast forward to today, though, where almost anyone can record a half-decent album in their garage. The cost of distribution is basically free, and people can purchase music by the song - no full album needed. And yet no one is stopping to ask why we still have twelve-song albums *(well, nobody but me, it seems).* We no longer primarily distribute music on LPs, but we still act as if we do. This is straight up **Legacide** - and it's thinking like this that I hope this book will train you to seek out, and eradicate.

Then of course there's a service like Twitter, I found a great interview with founders Biz, Ev, and Jack, from back in 2006.
legaci.de/twitterlunchmeat

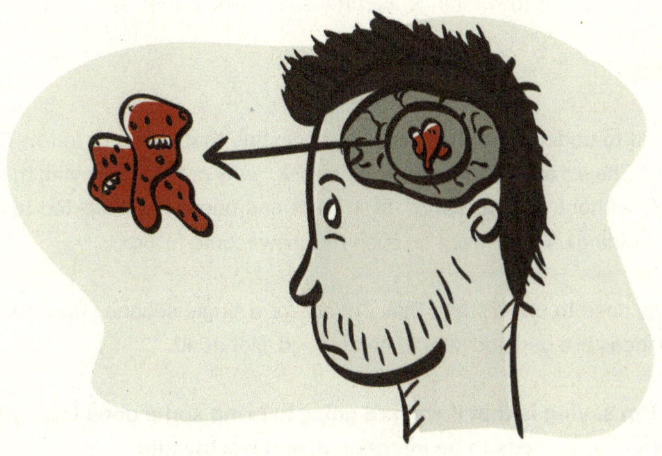

Here's how Jack Dorsey defined Twitter:

"**Twitter is the way to keep connected with your friends,** it's basically mini blogging with a low barrier to entry."

He went on to say:

"The other major constraint is we limit these to 140 characters so these are very short focused updates, and they're usually personal, and they're usually about just random things you're doing in the day."

Ev Williams continued,

"Another way that people put it is 'present-tense blogging'." He added, "Twitter for the most part is about what you are doing **right now.**"

And that made sense. If I wanted to tell my mates what I was up to, I'd send an SMS *(thus the character limitation)* to Twitter and everyone would know - a timeline worked perfectly. However, is that how we still use Twitter? Of course not, it's that too, but so much more. Do they still use the timeline that was put in place to solve a completely different problem? **Yes.** Could it be more effective if they re-thought it around its purpose today? Without a bloody doubt. Will they change anytime soon? Don't hold your breath...

Legacide.

You need to understand that I'm not suggesting that we don't follow George Bernard Shaw's advice to dream big and ask, "why not?". I'm saying that if we do that, without asking "why?" first, we'll find ourselves shackled to a past that is holding us back from an even more awesome future.

You also need to understand that I'm not for a single second suggesting that all old ideas are bad and should be dropped. Not at all.

What I'm saying is that if you are going to bring some good legacy thinking with you, it needs to be intentional, and worthwhile.

Twitter has, since the first writing of this, attempted a more dynamic timeline, however, it does seem to be a case of too little, too late.

Take transportation for example: way back when, if people needed to get from A to B, they used to use a horse and carriage.

Photo credit: www.historyplace.com

Then, finally, much to the joy of subjugated horses everywhere, came the motorcar. Now, if you look at the picture above you can clearly see that we did not actually *invent* ourselves a motorcar, but rather a simply created a *horseless carriage (I remember a penny dropping for me the first time I heard Brian Pinnock, Dimension Data's head of innovation, use this term).*

As 'revolutionary' as the invention of the car was, in its earliest iteration it was actually a lot more incremental and evolutionary than you might think. It really was just the horses that had been removed. I believe wholeheartedly that it was this very factor that made its adoption so smooth. Although cars were new, people understood them, they even understood the power conversion - **a four horse power engine could do the work of four horses**.

Smart.

[There is of course some degree of legacide in the usage of the term 'horse-power' today, as the numbers are now quite absurd, and thus largely useless as a literal comparison. Take my Triumph Street Triple R motorbike for example; it would need 106 horses if it wanted to generate the same amount of power back in the day.] that is around 1.6 tonnes of horse shit p /day

Often when it comes to innovative ideas we risk getting way ahead of the market, when all we really needed was to find a horseless carriage. More on this later, though.

So Legacide is not just a book about business, it's a book that presents a point-of-view and a way of thinking that will hopefully stick in your mind, spread to your business and then spill into many other aspects of your life. It may make you stop queuing for airplanes *(we did this before we had pre-seating - and, no, spending 2 minutes finding a space for your ridiculously large carry-on luggage does not warrant standing for 20-minutes in a queue)*, it may even make you question why you say "Bless you!" when someone sneezes *(thereby stopping the onslaught of the bubonic plague that was rife in 590AD through the use of prayer alone - and you see how well that worked for them)*. However, I hope I can **make you question** some of the big and important stuff, too.

Legacide is not a tough concept to get your head around - you should probably already have a fairly decent grasp of it by now *(if you don't, give this book back to your parents, kiddo - there's cuss-words coming)*. However sometimes we need a little bit of a hint as to where to start looking. The rest of this book is just that - a series of hints.

Now, turn the page...

You're getting warm...

warmer...

"Don't be afraid of new ideas. Be afraid of old ideas. They keep you where you are and stop you from growing and moving forward."

Anthony Robbins

NB!

LEGACY: BOOKS ARE SACRED

Why? Because they were expensive, because printing and distribution was expensive, because very few people could write, etc.

Books are the most precious knowledge resources we have - treat them with care, don't bend their spines and *(Shock! Horror!)* never, ever, ever make notes or scribbles in them!

Bullshit.

Books are tools. Use them as you see fit.

Write all over this one. Make notes, doodles and to-dos.

If there's something you like, highlight it. If there's something you hate, score it out. Dog-ear the pages if you want to come back to them *(legaci.de/dogear-rating)* - but, for goodness sake, if you do, then *actually* come back. If you're reading this on your Kindle, don't feel left out, you can do all these things too. That said, if you're anything at all like me, you're better off making notes in a notebook. I'd recommend the Writable *(www.humanwrit.es)* but then again, I'm biased.

Making a note is a special thing, it moves your brain from passive-consumer, to active-collaborator - you're making the book better, and to be honest, it needs a wee bit of help. **The more defaced a book, the more engaged the reader**.

The title of this section is **"NB!"** from the Latin Nota Bene, meaning note well. That's the one thing I ask from you - **note well**. And not just in this book - in all of them.

Just remember, notes are reminders. Reminders need attention to become action.
Ideas without action are nothing.
Make a mess, then do something.

BTW. While we're on the topic of defacing books, you should certainly check out "S" By J.J. Abrams *(Lost, Star Trek, Star Wars)*. The entire book takes place in the margins. Genius.
legaci.de/sthebook

your space to deface

I LOVE HATE

LEGACY: DO WHAT YOU LOVE

Why? Because Confucius said, "Do what you love and you'll never work a day in your life." Pfft... hippie!

If I'm to be completely honest with you, I'm something of an entrepreneurial snob. It frustrates me how everyone that starts a small business calls themselves an entrepreneur - being an entrepreneur has nothing to do with the size of your business, but rather to do with *the state of your mind.*

You see, most business people are driven by either talent or passion. Talented accountants start accounting firms, and people who love to own the latest furniture start a furniture store. Both these motivators can work, of course, but they're not particularly entrepreneurial.

A **small-business-minded person** walks into a flower shop one day to buy some flowers and loves it, so he buys a franchise and runs his own store. An **entrepreneur** like my mate Ryan, on the other hand, walks into a florist one day to buy flowers, gets frustrated by the act of having to physically go into a store, so he creates NetFlorist.

Entrepreneurs are driven by hate.

"That sucked, I can do it better", or "You know what's missing in your industry? I'll tell you, it's...". These are the mantras of the entrepreneur. To me, the number one most effective motivator for starting a business is frustration. Why not talent or passion? Because if you're passionate, you love it already and you'll probably change nothing. Where there's love, you'll find a ready product, where there's frustration, you'll find a ready market.

As for talent, well, the problem with this is that if you can do something yourself, you will - and limiting a business to selling your own time by the hour is a poor way to scale. If you make money selling your own time, you're a freelancer. Sell someone else's time, however, you have yourself a business.

Of course, I'm not suggesting that you *shouldn't* have talent or passion, just that they possibly shouldn't be your primary motivator.

In my mind, entrepreneurs do one of two things: We either FIX, or we FILL. That's it. **We look for things that are broken, or gaps that need filling.** Why? Because potential exists there. If you're not fixing or filling something, chances are you're replicating something. Don't worry though, the world is full of millionaire replicators but, fuck me *(that's an extremely important comma right there)*, you're missing out on all the fun!

If you want to have a chance of changing a little bit of the world, ignore the stuff you love, and take on the stuff you hate. There is nothing more empowering than looking at your business with an amateur's eyes. And don't think that you're throwing away your years of experience, you're not.

This could also simply be looking at processes within your current industry or job that piss you off. Where there's frustration, there's opportunity. Get angry.

P.S. I attended 99u in NYC and saw Cal Newport do a fantastic talk that echoed much of my thinking on this. I highly suggest you take the time to watch it.

legaci.de/calnewport

"Don't follow your passion. Let it follow you in your quest to create value for the world."

Cal Newport

THE SOLUTION TRAP

LEGACY: PROBLEM SOLVED!

Why? Because, dumb-ass, you've solved the problem. It means the problem, it's solved. Keep up!

Like I said, the best people and companies in the world are often driven by frustration - they solve problems. There's a big problem with problem-solving though, it's fekking expensive *(said in your best Irish accent)*, and isn't necessarily the 'end' you thought it was. You could well find yourself caught in a Solution Trap of your own making...

Think about it this way; when you set out to solve a problem, you're in a bit of a no-man's land. You don't know how much the project or innovation is going to cost and, more importantly, you don't know if anyone is going to want it when you're done. As an aside, this is why at this stage you should aim for MVP *(Minimum Viable Product)**.

However, you persevere and launch - and the market loves it. *Yaaay you!* This is the part where you start having fun and making cash, where you move from 'solve problem' to 'refine solution'. Your job now is to make the product better, get it out faster *(and cheaper)*, tweak according to market feedback - all those fun things. Eventually you'll get to version 2.0 and 3.0, each build better than the one before; slicker, sexier, faster, louder, nicer. The *_er* words are the hallmark of the solution refinement phase. There's no *_er* when you're first to market.

This, though, is when Legacide creeps in. You start seeing yourself as a company that is in the business of *Solution X,* as opposed to *Solving Problem Y.*

You keep trying to make your solution more *_er* in all the right places, yet the market just doesn't seem to be responding favourably, or at all, anymore... **Why?** Because you're now a cure for no disease. The original problem you set out to solve... guess what? You solved it! Now, your competitors copied you, there are more *_ers* out there than you can imagine and the whole thing has become a great big non-problem.

Look at that - you're stuck. In the Solution Trap.

I'm experiencing this now. When I started Missing Link *(as a presentation specialist firm)* in '97, if you wanted to do a preso, you had one tool: PowerPoint. You also had just one frame of reference, which was your teacher/lecturer's text-heavy overhead-transparency slide. So that's what we set out to do, build better PowerPoints.

That was the context of the problem we set out to solve, we did it, the market responded, our client base grew and grew and soon we were working with most of South Africa's top corporations. Our idea of progress was making a slide *faster*, making a strategy *better*, and for a *(long)* while, that was okay.

What about today? Are we facing the same problems? No we really aren't. Everyone's exposed to the latest TED talk or Apple launch. As for tools, there's Keynote, Prezi, Haiku, PowerPoint, SlideRocket and many, many more to choose from *(the last talk I did I made in a few hours in Haiku on my iPad mini)*. And yet there we are, still trying to sell better presentations like it's 1997. That's not bloody good enough.

If we want to move forward and get our business out of the *OK Plateau***, we need to be willing to make a sacrifice to the *Great Hungry Gods of Progress*. That sacrifice is, basically, our original solution.

We need to stop refining our old solution, and start solving a new problem.

Another great example of the Solution Trap for me is ticketing companies, the kind you use for concerts and the like.

In South Africa there's a service called Computicket. Today a person can log onto their functional *(albeit crappy)* site and buy tickets for most major concerts and events, but what problem did Computicket originally set out to solve?

Well, years back before Computicket came along, had you wanted to buy a ticket to see a production at the theatre, you would need to head all the way out to the ticketing office at the theatre itself and make your purchase. A frustrated problem-solver realised that this was flawed, and they set up connected kiosks in every major shopping centre, nationwide.

You could be sitting in one side of the country, and buy tickets for a concert taking place in two weeks time in another city altogether, from a location that was convenient for *you* - this was a major technological breakthrough.

Computicket made its cash by providing the venue with this convenience for a small percentage of sales. The primary problems they solved? Distance and time.

Let's look at today. Do we have a distance and time problem? No. Thanks, Internet! Yet venues still give a share of their revenue to a middleman that is servicing problems *(distance and time)* that no longer apply.

Today, it would be as easy for any venue to set-up their own white-labeled online ticketing system. They would own the database of theatre goers, they would be able to easily re-sell tickets for people that needed that service *(allowing them to draw more revenue)*, they could even sell additional services like pre-paid parking, and the re-sale of purchased tickets *(I'm giving this away for free, people)*.

And yet they don't. **Why?** Because selling tickets directly is simply not part of their thinking. Computicket does that for them *(for now)*.

At some stage, however, the venues will realise this - and where will that leave Computicket? Ask Kodak.

So, am I suggesting that these venues and promotors consider going it alone? Absolutely. Am I then suggesting the powers that be at Computicket call it a day? Absolutely not. I am, of course, suggesting *(strongly)* that they start solving a new problem - of which there are almost certainly many. Most importantly, I'm suggesting that they do it today. One way could be to provide self-managed white label versions of their tool to people all over the world. Another would be to open the tool to corporations planning internal events where no cash changes hands. What problem they choose to fix doesn't really matter - provided it's current, and real.

Right, I'm aware that this looks a lot like *Geoffrey Moore's Crossing the Chasm*** (you need to check this out)* and it is. It's just that Mulholland's chasm starts just after 'late majority' begins - it's the point at which your momentum starts waning. Don't get me wrong, you can make a fortune off the late majority - just consider Apple's sales *(the late majority, in Moore's curve is half the bloody market; Apple makes as much money from your gran's iPhone as it does from you, Mr. Trendsetter).* **Your job, though, is to start solving a new problem before the previous solution is obsolete.**

Let's look at Reed Hastings, the co-founder of Netflix *(we'll hear more about this dude later).* He avoided his own Solution Trap so well just years after he started the video rental giant to solve the problem of later return fees on films. If he thought like most of us, he would have stayed in love with his original idea of delivering videos by post for an unlimited period. He would have **refined his solution** by posting disks fast*er* with a great*er* footprint of distribution centres. And *somebody else* would have put *him* out of business.

He didn't do that though.

Instead he realised that with the advent of high-speed internet, the problem had moved from "post movies faster", "to stream movies better", thus he pivoted his business model towards the **new problem** of laggy downloads and is now the largest single consumer of bandwidth in the United States - his postal business discarded down to the hungry gods of progress.

It's hard, I know, but what got you here certainly ain't gonna get you there****, and as long as your focus remains on solution refinement, you're going to be stuck at the wrong side of the sacrificial pit. Just remember that you're not admitting that you were wrong, but rather understanding that you were right then.
legaci.de/bloodyrich

Ask yourself what problem you set out to solve, and go into detail ('make better presentations' doesn't cut it). Then ask yourself if it's still valid today. Better still, if you broke away from your current company and set out to solve a new problem for your industry, ask yourself what problem that would be - then solve that.
Fall in love with problems, not solutions.

* *Read Eric Ries' brilliant '**Lean Startup**' for more on MVP (who am I kidding, read the first two chapters - you'll be fine). NB. Don't let the title fool you, there's not a business around that doesn't need to read this.*

** *While you're at it, pick up a copy of Joshua Foer's '**Moonwalking with Einstein**'.*

*** *Oh, and '**Crossing the Chasm**'.*

**** *What the hell, let's go balls deep and pick '**What got you here won't get you there**', too. My, isn't Amazon going to do well today?*

LEGACY: RULES ARE RULES

Why? As we grow and develop, we figure things out. We develop a ruleset. This stops us from having to start from 'Go' again everyday. Rules, however, are made to be broken.

I'll tell you about the day I got that particular reality check. I run a successful firm out of Johannesburg, South Africa, that specialises in disseminating strategic messages to organisations. It's a niche industry, but one in which we are very highly regarded worldwide. We have a great client base and we deal with many of the biggest companies in the country, along with a good helping of multi-nationals. Sure they're big companies, but in our field, we're the smartest mo'fo's in the room.

In the 17 years that Missing Link has been around, we've developed a few rules and principles that we know will help you make your message stick. One of those is that we do not make any video *(corporate or otherwise)* last longer than 3-minutes - any more than that and you're boring people.

A few years back, we were working on a job for one of SA's big four banks. The client was on the way to us for a final approval and I could see my guys arguing with Sam, our then MD. I went over to see what was wrong and found out that the video we'd created for them had taken on a life of its own, and was sitting at **9-mind-numbing-minutes**! Horrors! We had no time to change anything and had to take the client through the monster we had created. The client, unfortunately, thought it was the best thing since interest rates and wasn't willing to cut anything...

I explained to them *why* it was too long. They didn't budge. I explained that in 10-years I'd never seen a video *that* long get a good reception. Still nothing. I suggested keeping all the content but cutting it into three, well structured 3-minute vignettes, broken up by a speaker offering context.
Even more nothing...

Eventually, out of frustration, I gallantly jumped on my high horse and told them that they could have the video as is, but I refused to take money for it. They insisted, but I stood firm, happy in my small victory *(I got home and told the missus - she laughed at me and called me an idiot. She was right, but that's besides the point).*

The next day, I made a point of attending the client's event, waiting for the 'I told you so' moment *(don't you love 'em?).* The video ran. At the 4-minute mark people were still attentive. At 5-minutes they were smiling. At 9-minutes the video ended and there were cheers from every corner of the room. **Me?** I was floored. The client took the stage and asked if they liked the video, the audience thundered back that they did. She then smiled, pointed at me and said, "Then you have to say thank you to Richard and the Missing Link team for creating their best video yet." I was under no illusion that she was actually having her own 'I told you so' moment. What a bitch! Who does that?

In hindsight, I can see what happened. This wasn't a run of the mill corporate video, it was about them, and no-one ever gets bored looking at footage of themselves; yet we tried to apply our one-size-fits-all rule where it didn't belong. I sheepishly thanked the client for the lesson, backed out the door and then bolted.

I got my ass handed to me by a banker. Epic fail.

I went straight back to the office, called everyone together and told them the new rule: "From now on, everything we know to be true about presentations, or anything else really, has a 10% margin for error. Any member of staff can invoke the 10% rule at any time to challenge the prevailing wisdom. So if I insist that slides should never have silly transitions, you can *'Invoke the 10'* if you think there's an instance in which it could."

And invoke it they did. Slowly at first, but increasingly as they saw the successful outcomes. That's when I noticed a funny thing - absolutely all innovation came from the 10%. You don't innovate when you know your method works, you simply improve - and I can tell you this, all the 'improvement' in the world counts for nothing when stacked up against something really new and cool.

How many things are you absolutely unwilling to budge on, and how many of those - if 'budged' - would make you better? I'm guessing that giving your team a little bit of wiggle room, when it can be properly justified, will open your eyes to some exciting possibilities within your business.

Allow your people to invoke the 10% rule. Better yet - do it yourself! The worst that can happen is that you try something new and fail - and learn. On the flip side, (more than) occasionally you'll change your world.

A MATTER OF PERSPECTIVE

LEGACY: INNOVATION GETS HARDER THE BETTER YOU GET

Why? Because when you're a market leader, who do you look up to?

You know the crappiest lesson I've learned since starting out? It's that the **one thing you lose as you grow in your career is your perspective.** And the bad news is that the loss of perspective is inversely proportional to the knowledge gained. It's as if you empty one cup in order to fill the other.

"In the beginner's mind there are many possibilities, but in the expert's mind there are few." *- Shunryu Suzuki*

It was this very thought that led us to branch into the field of innovation nearly 7-years ago, with our 21Tanks division.

As Missing Link, we kept getting asked to run innovation workshops for our clients - fixing problems, helping find the right idea, you get the picture - even though that traditionally wasn't our space. Now, innovation-problem-solving looked like a fun gig, so ran them we did - and for the life of us, we couldn't figure out why they worked so well. Until eventually it hit us; we realised that the one thing we categorically had over our clients was that we knew *very little* about the stuff they knew **a lot** about.

We brought *perspective* *(and a methodology - but that shit's more secret than the Colonel's original recipe).*

It turns out that perspective is the single most important ingredient in all of innovation. Elon Musk isn't a rocket scientist, and Orville Wright didn't have a pilot's licence, and that's exactly why they changed things.

You see, as you get better at your job, you develop tools, and the more you use those tools the better you get at wielding them. Which, unfortunately, makes you less likely to try anything else... Here's a quote for ya - one of my fav's: "If the only tool in your toolbox is a hammer, then every problem looks like a nail."

This is why your traditional consultants are failing you. They walk into your office with their power-suits and fatted-wallets, only to flip open their briefcases to show you their rocket-propelled, platinum-plated, solar-powered... hammers. Fancy yes, but also the very thing you already have by the bucket load.

This isn't rocket science. We all do it all the time when we leave dinner parties with solutions for other people's relationships but then get home and fall out with our spouse over who's making tea... You gotta love the clarity of the uninvolved *(more on this stuff later)*.

When you find yourself stuck, don't fret. Luckily for you perspective is never hard to find - just ask a few smart outsiders. Note, though, that this isn't about asking people what they think of your ideas, but rather how they would solve similar problems.

THE FALLACY OF BEST

LEGACY: BE THE BEST!

Why? Ego. And, because we think that's how we're judged...

"What's the best album of all time?", "What's the best restaurant in South Africa?"

I kinda believe that we have an unhealthy obsession with the concept of 'best'. I also believe that striving to be the best - unless you're a professional athlete - is missing the point...

"What's the best album of all time?" I'm not sure, The Beatles' White album, perhaps? Do I own it? No.
"What's the best restaurant in South Africa?" The Tasting Room in Franschhoek *(at the time of writing, anyway)*. Have I been? No.

Confused?

It's legacy-thinking to want to be 'the best'. Best is a bit of a holy grail. We all want it but not only is it hard to achieve, it's hard to quantify too. Everyone has a different idea of what best looks like, and it's something that we can, and do argue about.

What you should be trying to do is be the **favourite**. No one can argue about your favourite, it's an absolute. My favourite album of all time is 'The Fall of Ideals' by *All That Remains*. My favourite South African restaurant is Ghazal. My favourite local airline is Kulula *(international - Virgin Atlantic)*. Are they the best? Who gives a shit!? They're my best and, in my universe, that's what counts.

So why's this important? Well, you need to understand that the criteria for favourite is completely different to the criteria for best. The criteria for best is intellectual. For favourite: emotional. Here's the not-so-breaking news - we're emotional creatures, doubly so when it comes to making purchasing decisions. We strive to make the purchase that 'feels' right as opposed to the one

that 'is' right. Besides, the latter is generally too hard to quantify: best on whose standards? On what criteria?

Now, you may think that I'm arguing semantics, but not at all. Let's say you wanted to be the best restaurant in your city. Your to-do list would include the following:

- Best chef
- Best wine selection
- Top location
- Best decor/design

Even if you manage to get all these factors right, how long will it last? I can tell you how long: it will last until somebody gets a better chef, or a trendier location, or a...

Most importantly though, how often do you visit the best restaurant in your city? Once a year on a special occasion. And how often do you listen to the best album of all time? I'm betting very occasionally, basically when it plays on the radio.

Favourite though is a completely different story. My wife and I go to our favourite restaurant almost every week, and I listen to my favourite band all the time.

'Best' is a fickle mistress, and 'used to be best' is worth very little at all.

If you wanted to be the favourite restaurant for a group, on the other hand - let's say sushi lovers - your list could be:

- Great sushi chef
- LCD's displaying old ninja movies and Japanese game shows
- Japanese style photo booths
- Waitresses dressed in Kill Bill cat suits and tartan school uniforms
- Oh, and great sushi, of course

I can tell you this, if you appeal to your audience well enough, you'll get a lot more buzz from the Kill Bill chef than you will from your wine list. One important point though; if you want to be loved by one person, you have to be willing to be hated by someone else. Favourite doesn't live in the land of one-size-fits-all.

'Best' is tricky, and it's almost always open to debate, let's see someone try and argue with you about who you believe is your favourite author. It's impossible. **Favourite trumps best every time.**

Look at your business. What have you been trying to be 'best' at. Have you managed it and can you prove it? Now ask yourself if you're favourite at anything? Surprisingly, you're probably not. The good news is it's both more achievable and a shit-load more fun. Have a brainstorm, knock yourself out. If you come right, let me know, I'm always in the market for a new something-or-other.

BRAND BUILDING SHMAND SHMUILDING

LEGACY: YOUR LOGO IS YOUR BRAND

Why? Mostly because we misunderstand the term 'brand'. But also because we pay people to get all high and mighty about it.

Let's talk brand-building.

Designers don't design brands. At best, they create visual tools that help customers manage their expectations. A brand is simply the difference between that expectation and the experience that customer gets. It's the sum total of every interaction we have with a company, measured against the expectations we arrive with. This is the reason that when it comes to branding of any sort, user-experience trumps marketing every time.

I recently left a meeting at one of our banking clients. One of the attendees was with the dreaded brand police of the organisation, and she was arguing with me about a presentation slide we had created. She said that it was 'off-brand' *(what she meant was off CI - corporate identity, but who was I to argue?)*. I showed her a pic of a billboard in their CI manual that we had used as reference, she said that our design would be cool if it was on a billboard, but as a slide it was wrong.

This is of course non-sensical. Especially as the template that they wanted us to use was both ugly and, from a presentation point-of-view, ineffective! Aaarg!

I left frustrated *(could you tell?)* and went to an ATM on the way out to draw some cash. The ATM was dirty, it was offline, and all around the floor were discarded ATM slips *(now that's a legacy in and of itself)*. At the time I wondered if a photo of the ATM would be most, on-brand, on a billboard or on a slide.

Your corporate identity is not your brand.

I think it was Kidd Parker that said, "The only time a logo is a brand is when it's on a cow's ass". Another quote I love, this time by Rachel Sklar says, "Brand is not what you tell your customers - brand is what customers tell their friends."

Hell yes!

Missing Link has no corporate identity or fixed logo, and we change it as we see fit. There's no single element that's consistent other than the name itself... and, of course, the *experience* we give our customers. People are forever asking me how I'm able to run a business with no brand. I always reply with the same words: "We may have no logo, but we have a tonne of brand." When you remove all the window dressing, you have nothing to fall back on, except your product and the delivery thereof.

I'm not alone in this. Consider the world's highest ranked beer, Westvleteren. Westvleteren is brewed in a small town in Belgium by 5 Trappist monks *(5 more help with the bottling along with 3 secular labourers that assist with other tasks).* Despite demand being sky high, every year they sell just 1.4 million bottles. To buy them you need to call ahead on their "Beer Phone", pre-order, then visit the abbey yourself to collect your beer *(they don't sell to wholesalers or pubs).* You are also limited to just two cases per month, and they monitor this by tracking your phone number and licence plate.

The bottles are unlabelled, with all the required information being displayed on the bottle-top, and the full extent of their advertising campaign is the small signpost just outside the abbey, letting you know you've arrived.

Some would say the monks are successful despite themselves. I disagree. I think there are two elements to their success. The first is that the beer is obviously world class, the second is best described by the term coined by Stephen Brown in the great book "Free Gift Inside" - *marketease.* Nothing increases the perceived value of your product more than a little scarcity - of course that's not really the point of this section *(but do read Stephen's book).*

Westvleteren is reliant on making an amazing beer, and Missing Link has to keep creating kick-ass client experiences.

So what's the lesson here? Am I suggesting that you kill your corporate identity? No. What I'm suggesting is that you get your people to act as if it didn't exist. If you woke up tomorrow and logos were banned, you'd be forced to put all your effort into creating a better product. Once you got that right, you'd make sure that the delivery of that product was perfect - that would be your brand.

Look, you really do need to be worried about your brand, and you probably do need brand police. Just get them to worry about the real cases, and not just the parking violations.

legaci.de/giftinside

legaci.de/beermonks

DEADVERTISING

LEGACY: YOU NEED AN AD AGENCY

Why? How else was the world going to find out about your boring me-too product?

I'm a big fan of the TV show Mad Men. It features a group of ad guys in the golden years of the industry. Cigarette-smoking, whisky-swigging, womanising men that use their inherent creativity to sell the boring products of the day.

It's also one of the most depressing shows I've ever seen. **Why?** Because nothing has changed...

It amazes me that fifty years later, an industry that prides itself on being the creative geniuses of our day, are coming from one of the least evolved industries on the planet.

Creative director, copy writer, art director, client services. Every structure perfectly preserved as if in amber. The only noticeable difference is that the ties are gone *(and they now have to smoke outside)*.

And this is the industry you are relying on to help you sell your product. **WTF!?**

Stop it. Things have changed. Let me give you a wee example of how stagnant these guys are.

When adverts first graced televisions in the fifties and sixties, they lasted a nice round minute *(the first TV ad ever to run in the UK was for Gibbs SR toothpaste and it lasted 70-seconds)*. Over time though, given increased demand and decreased attention, these shrunk to the 30-second spots we see today.

This made a lot of sense - then. They were mini-stories, often with comedy. We'd watch the story and await the big logo reveal at the end. It worked. I'd also say in many cases it still does.

But not on YouTube.

Why is an industry that is so convinced of their god-like creativity, unable to see why the format for a thirty second TV ad, designed to be watched by an audience that is likely to sit through it, is perhaps no longer relevant for a generation that has a mouse hovering over the **Skip this ad in 5, 4, 3, 2, 1 *click*** panel? *(I think human reflex records would be broken daily if you timed how quickly we were clicking through to our desired vid - I mean, who wouldn't be in a rush to watch that German dude body slam into a frozen swimming pool?)*

legaci.de/poolslam

They have 5 seconds, and they know it. Yet they follow a fifty year old formula that requires us to wait to the end *(which we don't)* in order for us to see who is talking to us.

This is crazy. What they should be doing is tell us the story in the first 5 seconds *(it's worth mentioning that you only pay if they watch the full 30-secs)*. But I digress...

Look, do we still need these creative people? Sadly, yes, we do. We just don't need them for marketing or advertising. We need them for **product development**. You only need super smart marketing if your product is dull. If you take a fraction of the creativity you currently apply to advertising, and instead put that into the product and even process design, your customers will do the marketing for you.

Look at Uber. I doubt very much that a single person reading this is not familiar with this category-killing car service. Hey, most of you probably have the app on your phone right now. However, I bet you that none of you have seen, heard, or watched an Uber advert. How is this possible?

It's the same reason you never needed advertising to drive you to Google, and almost certainly it wasn't an award-winning advert that made you want that new iPhone. Sure, ads exist, however we all know you'd bought that shiny pocket toy long before you watched any commercial.

The marketing is baked in.

Consider this, if your advertising is winning awards, it's often because your product probably won't.

Okay so by now you'll be coming to the conclusion that the real legacy at play here is in fact boring product design. However it's just far more fun picking on the creative circle-jerk that is the ad industry, so bear with me a bit more.

Look, you should never trust a skinny chef. The first question you should ask your prospective agency is where they advertise. The only body of work you should be interested in is the advertising work they do to sell their own agency to clients like you. If they do, then great, but of course, they don't really believe in their own products so, at the very best, you will be shown some ego work that was posted in an industry publication showing how many awards they have won.

On top of that fact, your ad agency trades in the currency of those awards. You are funding their business development more than your own.

[Ever heard of 'scams'? That's where your agency runs ads that you haven't approved (or, often, actively condemned) without your consent, in obscure publications or at 3am on small-town radio stations, just so they can enter that campaign into awards - regardless of what that might do to your business. Ask Ford how they felt when JWT India did just that to them: legaci.de/adscam1. *The desire for peer recognition has overrun the desire to do the job you damn well pay them to do! Still not sure?*
Here's more: legaci.de/adscam2

In fact ask anyone in advertising about why they do what they do, and here's what you'll find: **Priority #1** - *win awards;* **Priority #2** - *sell product/build brands.*

Ban creative awards for any agency you use **immediately** - you are subsidising their marketing. If they do want to win awards for marketing, then the only product they should be marketing is their own, let them pay for their own paperweights.

Now, while I'm ranting, let's consider the term 'creative' for a minute, as in "I'm a creaaahtive". When someone says this to me I always ask them, "A creative what?" It's not a noun, ass-hat, it's an adjective. I'm also a creative person, so is my banker, my architect, the comedian I listened to last night, and the chef that prepared my dinner. South African business legend, Mark Lamberti, once told me that **he'd far rather hire an accountant that could play the piano than one that couldn't.** I love that.

Why then do advertising people believe that they have the sole mandate on being creative? Because we let them. And why do they insist on telling you that they're 'a creative'? I'll tell you why, because finishing the sentence is far too bitter a pill to swallow, "I'm a creative person that wishes I was a film director that now works in advertising selling cheque accounts for a large banking corporation."

Actually, let me take my earlier statement back. The advertising industry did manage one really good campaign in its day. It's the one where they convinced young, creative individuals that advertising is cool. One last thing, if you have a 200 strong marketing team, why do you also still need an agency? One is redundant.

phew

Okay, so rant over. Thanks for indulging me. I feel it's important to mention that most of my closest friends work in marketing, and I don't like them in spite of their jobs, but probably because of them. I just think that their talent is spent on the wrong things. Again, why design marketing for boring stuff when you could and should be helping your clients make remarkable products?

I've gone off on a wee tangent here, so let me summarise for you:
Point 1: Advertising sells products? No, better products sell products *(with a little help).*

Point 2: Ad agencies are the only ones who can get crazy? No, you should too *(read 'May Contain Nuts').*

Point 3: Advertising agencies are so far up their own arses that they no longer REALLY drive value for you - they do it for themselves. Change this.

If you're making boring stuff, stop it right now. Or change the way it's packaged, or even the way it's delivered. Change anything you like except your advertising. It's far better to differentiate with your product than your marketing.

If you get this right you can use your agency to amplify an already cool story. They'll be upset with you for stepping on their toes, but quite frankly, fuck 'em. If they want to be creative they should have gone to film school.

LEGACY: KEEP YOUR EYE ON THE COMPETITION

Why? Yeah, I'm stumped here. I can see no really good reason why we're so completely obsessed with our competition.

Okay, so strictly speaking, you should probably still keep an eye on the competition, but just one - and only occasionally. See, the truth of the matter is, from an innovation standpoint, chances are the real innovation ain't going to come from them... or you.

Let's look at one of may favourite business rivalries. No, not Pepsi vs Coke, and not Mc'ds vs. Burger King - Visa vs MasterCard. The single most pointless rivalry in business history.

Hey, Visa! Hey, MasterCard, I have a secret to tell you...

Nobody gives a crap!

Seriously, we couldn't care less. If it wasn't for those drop down menus in website shopping carts, we wouldn't even know which one of you we're with. You see, my credit card relationship is with my bank *(tenuous, sure)*, not you. I have never in my life walked into a store that accepts one of you, and not the other. Maybe they exist, I've just never seen them.

It's not even my choice for goodness sake, *my bank makes that for me.* And yet, still you advertise. If you guys want to save a fortune, the CEOs of your two companies should go to lunch and decide to cancel all marketing immediately.

An even better idea would be to spend the marketing cash on product development, which you have largely ignored. Let's face it, it's inconceivable that I'll carry a credit card in my wallet 20 years from now - 10 is probably a stretch, and yet you're nowhere in this regard. It's companies like the coffee shop Starbucks that are innovating in this regard, allowing me to pay for my cuppa with an app. Now that I trust them for that, what's to stop them rolling their tech out to other retailers? Star*bucks* indeed. Hell, even the co-founder of Twitter is closer than you two, what with his "Square" thingamabob.

If you are not shitting yourself, you should be!

So, Visa and MasterCard have spent so much time looking over the wall at each other that they never bothered to consider that the real competition may come from elsewhere. They're certainly not alone in this.

Working on many presentations over many years for many industries *(financial services, FMCG, you name it)*, it amazes me how often these guys look no farther than their peers for innovation and/or inspiration. Even more strange is that they only ever measure themselves against their industry competitors. I find this extraordinarily short-sighted, even if you find innovation there, you'll always just be next to bat. **You want to be first.**

Take Netflix for example, co-founder Reed Hastings found himself looking elsewhere for answers:

"I had a big late fee for 'Apollo 13.' It was six weeks late and I owed the video store $40. I had misplaced the cassette. It was all my fault. I didn't want to tell my wife about it. And I said to myself, 'I'm going to compromise the integrity of my marriage over a late fee?' Later, on my way to the gym, I realised they had a much better business model. You could pay $30 or $40 a month and work out as little or as much as you wanted."

So he did it. He augmented the model of one industry with that of another, and made a fortune doing so, leaving his legacy competitors in a frantic fight for survival.

Would Blockbusters have looked to a health club for the answer? Of course not. They looked simply at the other video stores.

This is why so many established industries are destroyed by ignorant upstarts.

The truth of the matter is that the innovation doesn't always exist within your current paradigm. However, there's a good chance that it already exists in a different one. It's your job to find it.

The thing is, we all do it. My good friend Howard Mann (author of The Business Brickyard) calls this Nemesis Theory, and his strategy to get around it is great:

Step one: *Write down everything you know about your competition (oh, I'm no longer just talking to Visa and MasterCard, this means you, punk)*
Step two: *Throw it away*
Step three: *Write down everything you know about your customers, ask yourself what they will be doing 10 years from now. Be honest - chances are, in most industries, it'll be pretty far from what they're doing today*

Then ask yourself what problems your current customers may have with your industry today, or what issues you have in your service delivery to them. Create a list of at least five completely different industries that faced similar problems. Task your managers to research how those industries tackled them. My guess is that you'll be just a hop, skip and jump away from the next big breakthrough in your industry if you do, even if it's just old news elsewhere. Especially if it is, actually.

Don't let a coffee shop put you out of business, it's very embarrassing.

SLAY THE GREATS

LEGACY: OLD TRUMPS NEW

Why? Because we study the classics in order to get a better understanding of how our civilisation has been shaped, and thus revere them.

I read recently that Citizen Kane *(1941)* is no longer rated as the best film of all time. Upon recent review, it was knocked from the top spot by Alfred Hitchcock's Vertigo *(1958)* - this is in and of itself a fairly absurd idea as nothing about the two films has changed... *legaci.de/downwithkane*

This was from a list of the Top 50 Greatest Films of All Time - What strikes me as odd is how much we seem to have regressed in our film making quality. Believe it or not, of all films created in the 21st Century, only two; In the Mood for Love *(2000)* and Mulholland Dr. *(2001)* managed to make the list at all. legaci.de/greatestfilms

This is stark contrast to the highest-grossing films of all time, a list topped by the likes of Avatar *(2009)* and Titanic *(1997).* legaci.de/topgrossing

Now, I'm not suggesting that Avatar is necessarily a better film than Vertigo, however, I would suggest there's a degree of legacide in the original list. **Why is this?** Because we are unable to slay our idols when in fact, that is exactly what we should be doing.

It is inconceivable that we have not improved over time, yet no one challenges the classics.

Why is this relevant to your business? If we still think that great business practice put in place by Jack Welsh in the eighties is the greatest thing since sliced bread, then we may find ourself applying a strategy in this year that was created for a different world. And I'll bet that there's a good chance you have found yourself quoting the business greats like Branson, Ford, Peters, Jobs, etc. in your last presentation decks, when there are some amazing minds just starting out now who are more relevant for today.

Hit Google and do a search for guys like Jason Fried, Elon Musk, and Tony Hsieh - these are the guys people will be quoting 20 years from now. It's their thinking that will take you forward. The greats, as amazing as they are, run the risk of keeping you stuck in the present.

(startupquote.com is a good place to start.)

"We can't understand the future or the present until we have some sort of grappling with the past."

Martin Scorsese

IE6 & THE CASE OF ANTI-LEGACIDE

LEGACY: IF WE CHANGE OUR STANDPOINT NOW IT'LL BE A PR NIGHTMARE

Why? Nobody wants to admit that they're wrong.

Here's the scenario: you've spent the last few years singing the praises of your latest product or service. You've stood in boardrooms and presentation halls telling people why it's the answer. Now, years later, I'm telling you that you should start telling people that that's no longer the case - that's going to kick off a PR shit-storm. Right?

Actually, quite the opposite.

In 2001 Microsoft launched their latest browser, IE6, with much fanfare. Terms like "Get more from the web" and "added DHTML enhancements" were used to describe it. However, that was over a decade ago. The web changed, and Microsoft knew it. Understandably, I was a little *(a lot)* surprised to see a tweet from @microsoft in 2011 that read:

"It's not often that we encourage you to stop using one of our products, but for #IE6 we'll make an exception."

The tweet contained a link to http://www.ie6countown.com, a site that was dedicated to the demise of this once iconic browser. The text on the site read:

10 years ago a browser was born.

Its name was Internet Explorer 6. Now that we're in 2011, in an era of modern web standards, it's time to say goodbye.

This website is dedicated to watching Internet Explorer 6 usage drop to less than 1% worldwide, so more websites can choose to drop support for Internet Explorer 6, saving hours of work for web developers.

Do you think there was a PR shit-storm? Not at all. There was a storm though, and it was a veritable hurricane of good PR for a forward-looking brand.

Microsoft knew that their browser was obsolete, they just decided on being proactive with letting you know that, too. Don't you think that your customers would prefer to hear the same from you? To me, this example of anti-Legacide has positioned the software giant as innovators and forward thinkers - that could be you. Is your product long in the tooth? If so, build something better, then climb to the roof of your corporate empire and tell the world that you're putting the old one out to pasture. You can have fun with it too. If I was Microsoft, I would have thrown IE6 a retirement party, given it a gold watch and left it to live out its golden years in peace. That's just me though.

THE BIG BOYS KNOW BEST

LEGACY: LEARN FROM THE LEADERS

Why? Experience is a tricky thing to let go of. If it worked for me there, it should work for me here.

So, you've done your time in the corporates and you're sick of 'paying the man'. Who does he think he is? Getting all the money, while you do all the work *(you're wrong, but let's leave that for another book).* It's time you went out on your own!

And that's exactly what you do. **Fab!**

Before you go any further, though, I want you to take a lesson from my mate, Josh.

Josh worked for me at Missing Link for a good few years. He's a smart guy though, and he knew at the time that Missing Link was a stepping stone. His end goal was advertising *(Shock! Horror!).* So he left and went to work for a small specialised ad agency in Jo'burg. He picked this agency because of its entrepreneurial flair. The founder, after having done his time in the Majors, decided to change things up and start a smaller, niched agency - this appealed to our hero.

After a few months, Josh and I were having lunch and he told me a story that blew my mind. He was in a meeting one day in his capacity as the client services guy, along with him was one of the art directors. They sat patiently through the client's brief before heading back to the office, promising the client that they would revert with a mock-up in a day or two.

The next afternoon, Josh went over to the art director and said, "Dude, where are we with mockups?" The guy looked back at him with a dazed expression, "Uuh Josh - I didn't start them yet, I was waiting for a brief from traffic." Now traffic was a single dude *(as in one person, he may have been in a relationship, I'm not sure)* whose job it was to schedule the various projects, it's worth noting that traffic was not in the original brief. Josh was supposed to brief traffic on the project, and traffic would in turn brief the very guy that was sitting next to Josh in the client meeting. **Makes perfect sense really.**

Josh was indignant, "But you were in the meeting with me - you got the brief first hand." "Yeah," replied the AD, "but that's not how it works in an agency."

And it's not. At least it's not in big agencies with all their moving parts. However, Josh's company was not a big agency, far from it.

So let's say you're like Josh's boss, you had worked in a large company for most of your career, you would have been exposed to many practices that were imperative to the successful running of a company of that size. When you have a juggernaut of a business, procedure is critical. You can see why practices like this would have been carried across without much thought. I think that's the problem, when you start-over you have the luxury of being able to pick and choose the bits that could work for you, and that's what you should do.

Now don't get me wrong, I'm all for procedure, but what we have here is a case of taking a step that is required in a big 50+ person company, and adopting it in a small business of 10 people, where it's simply a hinderance. Too often we adopt policies from the companies we paid our dues in, when in fact one of the biggest advantages of starting your own business is liberating yourself from these constraints.

Your biggest single advantage when you are one of the little guys in a world full of giants is your agility, your ability to move unconstrained by policies and procedures designed to keep companies of size on the straight and narrow.

Think about it this way, if you're building a bungalow, you wouldn't lay a foundation that would support a skyscraper - this is very similar.

Have a look at the processes you brought with you from your previous company; you don't have to take them all, only the ones that work for your new reality. If you're starting smaller, find out if you can re-jig them to make more sense in a firm of your size. Oh, and if you're in a big firm, ask if the tech available to us today could perform tasks like these with more efficiency. You'll probably be pleasantly surprised.

Remember, your goal is to be different to the firm you came from, and not just smaller.

EXCEED? BREAK!

LEGACY: THE WAY TO GET GOOD WORD OF MOUTH IS TO EXCEED OUR CUSTOMERS' EXPECTATIONS

sorry, i just vomited a little

Why? Well this one is pretty easy. We know we will be measured on a customer's expectations, and if we fail in this regard, they are pissed. So if we want to please them then doing the opposite makes sense. It does, but is having 'pleased customers' really enough?

'Exceeding expectations' is a platitude, and it's for amateurs. Why? Because even when we do, we're still simply doing our job, albeit fairly well.

It would be far more powerful to break their expectation-engine *(put this book down and read - Made to Stick or* legaci.de/learnWoM *now).* You see, everyone comes pre-loaded - they know what they think they're getting. They expect it. If you mess with that expectation though, you either win big, or lose horribly...

A few years back I was doing a job in Doha, in the Middle East. We were staying at the Four Seasons *(amazing hotel, by the way).* When we checked in, I remember telling the receptionist, Achmed, that I was craving a chocolate and asked if my room had a minibar. He looked at me with a grin and proudly replied "This is the Four Seasons, sir, every room has a mini-bar."

Then he checked something on the computer, frowned, and said, "It seems that house-keeping is still busy in your room, would you mind waiting a few minutes?" I said that that would be no problem and took a seat. *(He'd send my bags up in the meantime and got me a drink.)* A minute later he picked up the phone, mumbled, listened for a second before leaning the phone on his shoulder and telling me, "Mr. Mulholland, thanks so much for your patience, your room is ready for you now. Please do enjoy your stay at the Four Seasons."

Off I went up to my room where I discovered, on the desk, a two-tiered tray of Belgian chocolates next to a hand-written card that said "With compliments - Achmed".

WTF?!

I was speechless.

He could have charged me, but I wouldn't have shared this story with *(to date)* thousands of people if he had. He could even have let me come up to my room and sent them up afterwords. **But no, he understood the value of unexpected surprise and delight. A small delay for a big impact.**

The Four Seasons could spend $1000 on a more comfortable bed. That may well have been 'exceeding expectations', but really, at a five-star hotel, I expect a five-star *(i.e. crazy awesome)* bed. No, what they did instead was spend $20 and a little initiative on breaking my expectation-engine - that's something I'll remember forever.

The Four Seasons didn't exceed my expectations, they kicked the shit out of them.

You need to stop trying to simply give your clients and customers (and spouses etc.) a better version of what they expected. They'll be happy, but not surprised. You need to hack their prediction-engines and create moments of "un-expectation" that they'll remember forever.
Remember this well:
Good service is defined on how well you do your job. Great service is defined by how well you do your "not my job".

TIMING IS EVERYTHING

LEGACY: BEEN THERE, DONE THAT

Why? We touch a hot oven plate when we're a kid, and we very quickly learn not to do it again. This is a process that has kept us alive.

Every one of us knows a person that will tell you that they had the idea for some greatly successful innovation years before it got big *(I personally came up with the idea for Google while suckling my Mum's left boob sometime in early '75)*. That's the thing though, you have to innovate at the right level for the market, at the right time.

One of my business heroes is Nissan CEO, Carlos Ghosn. You could write a whole book on smart things that this guy has done *(it would be a crappy idea though, someone beat you to it)*.

One of these such stories goes like this: just after taking over at Nissan, Carlos asked to see the car designs that had been rejected in the past few years.

He took two designs out of the reject pile and told his team that he was going to manufacture them. One was the next generation Z-car, the other, the X-Trail.

The X-Trail went on to become the best selling car in its class, and the 350Z *(after a 6-year hiatus of all Z-car production)* was an international hit. It was these two cars, the unwanted vehicles in the discard pile, that put Nissan back on the map.

A few years back my folks bought me the '*Waking the Dead*' box set for my birthday. '*Waking the Dead*' is a great British cop show, not unlike CSI, except here the detectives solve cold-cases using new technology. The theory is that at the time the crime was committed *(years and years ago)*, we didn't have the cool gadgetry that we have now. Week after week, the guys pull out a virtual toy-shop of tech to get the job done and solve old cases.

Like I said in the intro to this book, when we innovate we tend to look forward. This is cool, but I'm not sure if it's always the best plan of action. **Sometimes it may be worth solving the cold cases.**

Imagine if Apple users wrote off all PDAs after the Newton - we wouldn't have the iPad. Or, worse still, imagine we were put off by the first generation of eBook readers *(SoftBook: 1998, just so you know)* - I'd be seriously lost without my Kindle...

My favourite example here is a lot more recent, though. Have you heard of Ryan Grepper? Didn't think so. Ryan Grepper is an entrepreneur that has a business that turns over around 13 million dollars. That may not seem special to you, until you understand that he only properly started trading in July 2014. Well, sort off... ***Let me explain:***

In December 2013 Ryan set up a Kickstarter campaign for a product that he'd invented. It was a good product but, unfortunately, in spite of the fact that it managed to raise $110k *(no mean feat for a Kickstarter campaign)*, he didn't manage to reach its $150k funding goal. In short, he failed. After this, 90% of us would have given-up, but not this guy. Just 9 months later he was back, this time with a slightly better product. This time around he was successful, raising over $13m in pledges in just one month! What was he selling? A cooler box. A fancy one, true *(bluetooth speakers, a blender, the works)*, but yeah - a cooler box.

So what changed?

Turns out not a huge amount. Just enough, really.

Firstly, the season changed *(timing, people, timing!)*, a definite factor in Ryan's product. Then the funding goal changed. This time Ryan only needed to raise $50k, an amount he was confident he could reach, given the backers he attracted last year.

These backers gave him momentum out of the gate that caught the eyes of the media, and so it started.

The most important point here is that Ryan is not successful in spite of his earlier failure, but **because of it!** Had he done slightly better the first time around and managed to make his $150k, well he would simply be another forgotten, albeit marginally successful inventor. Instead, he is the second most-successful example of crowd-funding to date, *(at the point of his campaign, he was the most successful)* and will surely use this to build a serious business.

Here's the plan, have a look at ventures or markets that were ignored, or even failed in the past. Give them a second look.

1) You're seeing them with fresh eyes... and fresh eyes are good
2) As a species, we may struggle to learn from the mistakes of others, but we're pretty good at learning from our own. You go into the project a little older, and a lot wiser.
3) It's a whole new world out there. Could be you were just way ahead of your time (you're smart like that).

"Been there. Done that." may not be as final as you think.

BAD FIRST ITERATIONS

LEGACY: IT SUCKED THEN, SO IT MUST SUCK NOW

Why? The hot-plate again, of course.

Of course, thinking about timing is not limited to the things we do in our business, but also the tools we use. When it comes to trying new things, there isn't much that is quite as destructive as the phrase, "We tried that before." Yet there's hardly a week that goes by where someone or the other doesn't say just that.

A few years ago I was snowboarding in Austria. I've always used standard Burton bindings and have been happy with them, it's just a bit of a pain 'strapping up' after every lift. Enter *Flow* bindings. You just step in, pull one lever and you're riding. Sorta...

The problem with the original Flows were that they were not a tight fit at the front *(which you need to not-die)*, so most people tried them once, then wrote them off. The Flow guys clearly aren't idiots so, within one season, they'd added a second lever and you now have a perfect fit - problem solved! Yet many *(without trying the new and improved product)* will still say, "Flows don't sit as tight as regular bindings." I own some. Those people are wrong.

You hear this kind of argument all the time. Take automatic cars: I personally can't stand manual/stick shift, but I'm forever being told that automatic cars aren't as fast to shift, and that you have more control driving stick.
Seriously? Welcome to 10 years ago, buddy. Jump into any Mercedes AMG, with automatic transmission, wait for the light to turn green, put your foot down, and tell me you'd prefer to change gears manually. I prefer holding on for dear life.

Just because an idea, whether it's a product or even a business model, wasn't as successful as we'd hoped when we first tried it, doesn't mean that it will always be the case - sometimes, with minimal tweaking, something will go from awkward to awesome, and you'll never know... Years ago I tried an early beta of a calendar service called tungle.me. It was a great idea, but a bit buggy, and a bug when managing appointments with clients is a deal breaker. embarrassing! So I stopped tungeling. Six months later, I went back to it and gave it another try and you know what? They heard about the bugs, fixed 'em and provided exactly what I was looking for.

[Six months later still they were bought out and closed; try doodle.com. You're welcome.]

Go back to your dusty, little bag of tricks. Think about things you've used over the last few months or years; those things where the idea itself showed potential, but the execution wasn't up to scratch. Give them a second chance. And, when it happens again with something new you're trying, earmark the tool for 'Try in 6 months', I can't tell you how many times this has proven worthwhile to me. You need to beware the nay-sayer that shoots something down because "you tried it a few years back" - better still, don't be that guy.

Maybe it's about time that you tried something old (which, coincidentally, is exactly how I landed my 30 year-old wife).

APPLE & THE COOLING FANS

LEGACY: WINNING FORMULAS

Why? When we start, no one knows us. If we do one thing that makes us famous, it's easy to start believing that that one thing is the very foundation of our business, when in fact it may just be what got us noticed.

I was lucky enough to watch The Woz speak at the Creativity World Forum in Belgium a few years back, he recounted a story that has stuck with me ever since.

So back in the day Apple had a problem: they knew they needed to make their computers smaller, but they also needed to dissipate all the heat that their advanced processors were producing. Thus it was the size of the fans that was the biggest constraint to progress.

Along came one of their designers with an idea for a completely fanless computer which would use various heat dissipation techniques to get around the problem. Jobs loved it, and soon Apple had revolutionised the personal computer space with their fanless machines. The mantra from then on was **"No fans!".** *(Ironically, the lack of fans increased the amount of Apple fans, but let's leave the bad, obvious puns for someone else's book.)*

This was good news if you were Apple or one of their users *(but really crap if you were in the business of manufacturing fans).*

Fast forward a few years, add a bit of Moore's law, and you'll understand why Apple found themselves facing the same predicament again. The processors were so fast that the heat dissipation systems could no longer keep up. R&D approached Steve with a new, smaller fan that could do the job, and he refused.

"...put what you do in front of how you do it."

"*We* don't use fans!" he said.

This carried on for a long time until, one day, someone said to him, "Steve, I just want to check - are we in the 'building fanless computers' business, or are we in the 'building small and sexy computers' business?".

...and now Apple have fans.

There are a few lessons here, the obvious is always to put **what you do** *in front of* **how you do it**. *However, I also love that the fan companies took the well needed kick in the ass and ran with it. If the market tells you your product is obsolete, you can argue with it, or you can hit the drawing board fast.*

BACK TO THE FUTURE

LEGACY: ASKING THE WRONG QUESTIONS OVER AND OVER AGAIN, HOPING FOR A DIFFERENT RESULT

Why? I have nothing... Because we're pig-headed I guess, and often narrow minded.

Because there's nothing wrong with us, so if we ask the questions for long enough, the answerers will get it.

When I was a kid, I used to love watching legal TV shows. A bad-ass prosecutor would berate a witness with the same angry questions over and over until the defendant's attorney jumps out their chair shouting, "Objection your honour! Asked and answered!"

Well, hot damn. Many a meeting I've found myself wanting to shout this at our clients. Let me explain...

Do me a favour and take a second to answer the following question:

Q: When will cars be able to fly?

- ☐ 5 years
- ☐ 10 years
- ☐ Never
- ☐ They already can, I'll have mine in pink

When I ask this question in my talks, I usually get a lot of 1's and 2's. The truth of the matter is that if you'd answered 4, you would be right. Cars can fly; a company called **Terrafugia** has done it.

Why, then, do we all think that this invention exists somewhere in the distant future? Basically, it's because we have a fairly complex idea of what a flying car should look like *(you can thank Marty McFly and Co. for this)*. We want boosters, vertical lift off, sleek silver designs. We want to see our dream sports car without wheels. In other words, we have absolutely no idea what a 'flying car' actually is.

The question, "How can we make cars fly?" is a complex one that people have asked and struggled with for years. If I asked you to figure it out, it would take a while *(if you got it at all)*. However, I think Terrafugia probably tackled this in a different way. My guess is that they realised that we already have the whole flying thing worked out, so the question they asked was probably a lot more like this:

How do we make planes drive?

This question is a lot easier to figure out. I tested it on a group of teenage boys from King Edward school in Johannesburg, and it took all of 90-seconds before someone piped up, "Fold the wings away when you're driving".

...and that's exactly what Terrafugia did:

(Look, I'm the first to admit that the Terrafugia ain't perfect... it's hardly a panty-dropper. But hey, it's a start.)

Strangely enough, we solved the problem of flying, historically speaking, not too far after we solved the problem of driving, the issue with flying cars was never actually about figuring out how to make things fly - it was simply an issue of practicality, but that wasn't obvious until the question was changed.

If you've been struggling for ages with a problem in your business, take some time to try and reframe the question. Believe it or not, the most effective way to get a different answer to a problem is not to keep bashing away at it - your brain needs a new set of starting blocks.

Next time you have a big problem to deal with, ask the question 3 different ways to 3 different groups - you'll be amazed at what you find.

Stop sweating the answers...

Ask. Better. Questions!

("Objection, sustained.")

THE DANGER OF THE BEAUTIFUL MUNDANE

LEGACY: WE MUST FOLLOW BEST-PRACTICE

Why? Because way back when we lacked the ability to track what people do at an individual level. We couldn't get specific, so we watched them holistically.

Years ago, when we started Missing Link, we weren't very good. Our guys knew their way around an edit suite, but we generally just relied on fun, no-frills videos that showed our clients doing silly things - and they loved us for it.

As we've grown up we've got a whole lot better. We now know how to set up lights, what the correct audio levels are, which voice artists are good, etc. Now our videos are beautiful, but that doesn't make them better! In fact, they're often boring. And that's not okay. We got confused by the word best, in 'best-practice'.

I call this the **beautiful mundane,** and I get to see the beautiful mundane a lot. People spend a fortune making a really sexy version of something that, at its core... is still dull *(thus, ineffective)*. There's a word for this, it's "nice".

Nice is acceptable, but unremarkable.

Let's take offices as an example - I see people spend an absolute fortune on furniture, artwork, water-features and pot-plants. In theory, they get everything right but, in the end, they look pretty much like every other company in their market.

People need to forget nice, and focus rather on different.

“...forget nice, and focus rather on different”

The upside is that **different** is often cheaper, and you have more fun coming up with it. At Missing Link we have good-enough desk chairs, but we've had a skateboard ramp, a stripper pole, a deli designed like a morgue *(complete with body parts and our own corpse - his name's Chris).* And today our office is so out-of-the-ordinary that it was a category winner in Inc. Magazine's **'World's Coolest Office Awards'.** You should pop in, we're all kinds of awesome.

We could have spent the cash on a better-than-good-enough desk chair, but no-one would have thanked me for it. It may not be the most functional, but for years I worked from a queen-size bed in an office themed like a kid's bedroom. I loved it, and my clients loved it - now I'm in a treehouse.

Take a look at your products, look at your surroundings, look at the coffee and biscuits you serve your clients (look at everything). If you see something that's "nice", change it.

GOLDILOCKS INNOVATION

LEGACY: WE *NEED* TO INNOVATE TO THE EDGES

Why? Improvement is a simple concept to understand. Start with one thing, do it better, measure and repeat. There's a lot more to 'innovating though' than 'improvement'.

There's a race on out there. It's fast, it's furious, and it's pretty damn relentless - it's a race to be the '_est'. That could be the biggest, the smallest, the fastest, the thinnest. Once that race starts, there's no stopping it.

And that's a very real problem. So often we see companies blindly pursuing a specific innovative pathway, only to find that they've left practicality behind them. It's a fine line really - too **close** to your customer's expectations, and you're just more-of-the-same; too **far** and you're not practical - we need to aim for the Goldilocks innovation, the 'just right'.

Take USB thumbdrives. For ages, if you played in this space you had to do two things simultaneously; make the capacity bigger, and make the drive itself smaller.

Then along came LaCie, they developed the keydrive, a USB "key" that is literally that, a rugged metal-housed key-shaped device that sits inconspicuously on your keyring - except this key holds your data. This is the perfect size.

It feels 'just right' for the consumer *(sure, Verbatim have much smaller colourful plastic drives now, but they break, get lost, and are generally clumsy for big fingers).* Once you hit 'just right', I no longer care about 'est' anymore. The upside to this is, of course, that as soon as you reach that particular innovative Goldilocks point, you're free to innovate along a different path *(in LaCie's case - capacity).*

Mobile phones did the same thing: do you remember the iconic ad by Ericsson years back, with their tiny phone sitting next to a teacup? They over-innovated. We knew phones were too big, so we set out to make smaller phones as opposed to small-enough phones. Of course the current generation of *Phablets (WTF!?)* have completely over-shot Goldilocks yet again.

These guys just can't seem to get it right. "My phone is too thick", said no iPhone 5 user ever. "My battery sucks", says all of them, and yet Apple *(and Samsung, and everyone else)* keeps making thinner phones instead of bigger batteries. This is like going to the doctor for a head-ache and getting your colon irrigated. **Goldilocks people, damn it!**

Most recently we've seen this happen with the frame rate on TVs. I have one of those state-of-the-art, badass Samsung TVs with the 3D and gesture control. It's amazing. Too amazing, in fact... Is the quality highest? Yes. Do I enjoy it? Bloody no. Everything looks like it was shot as a soapie or made-for-TV film. Sure the quality makes things lifelike, but with 'lifelike' we lose our suspension of disbelief - you can almost see that things are props. **Reality, it turns out, is not really what we want from a good film, rather we want to escape from it for 90-minutes** *(and we're not used to it, and it's nasty).*

Time may prove me wrong here, but as I write this, Peter Jackson is busy adamantly defending his decision to shoot The Hobbit in 48 frames per second *(as opposed to the usual 24)* after very mixed reviews at the preview streaming. I can't personally see this ending well.*

The lesson here is this: *know when to stop moving in a specific direction. Remember, you're rarely trying to create the 'est' product, you're trying to create the 'just right' one, that's still a few steps ahead - the Goldilocks one. Once you get there, stop, and apply all your innovative resources in a different direction. Oh, one thing though: first you need to have a good idea of what 'just right' feels like, but it's usually not that difficult.*

*Update - pretty much everybody hated it - quality schmality.

"We can't know where we're going unless we know where we've been."

Martin Scorsese

FILLING TIME

LEGACY: MEETINGS LAST AN HOUR

Why? Habit.

Let's say I called you up to see if you were free for a meeting next week. I'd offer a few options of times that I could do and, when we agreed upon one that worked for us both, you'd open your calendar app and create a meeting. How long would you allow for that appointment?

My bet is that 97% of you would create one that lasts an hour.

Which, when you think about it, is quite strange, as meetings don't have to take an hour - we just think they do.

Our time is based on the Babylonian number system, a system devised to be divided up into a maximum amount of increments, thereby allowing us to utilise time in many ways. Think about it: in that 'hour' we could have three 20-min meetings, two 30-min meetings, four 15-min ones... you get the picture. And yet, we click and drag for an hour every time.

Parkinson's Law states that **"Work expands so as to fill the time available for its completion".** So if you've *allowed* an hour, it will *take* an hour.

I remember years ago when I was a lighting tech, I was on tour with UB40 *("THUD" - ah yes the ever-so-sweet sound of a dropped name).* The first show was in Durban and took us a full day to set-up, and we were working hard and smart. When we arrived in Pretoria for show number two, the trucks with the gear... didn't. Panic set in as everyone frantically tried to find the missing trucks in a time without vehicle tracking and cellphones. Eventually they arrived at 1am on show day, leaving the lighting crew just five hours to do what took us around 18 hours on the gig before. Yet, we did it. By sunrise the rig was up and the lights were focused and programmed.

That's not the remarkable bit though, the really big deal here is that when we went to show number three in Cape Town, it yet again took us a full day. It didn't feel like we were wasting time, or working slower, we just worked according to the time allotted.

And that's exactly what happens in almost every meeting I've ever attended.

There's a second law *(made up by me)* that says that "All meetings are not created equal". Thus they should not be allocated an equal time.

So here's my suggestion, maybe grab a coffee quick, this is gonna get wordy...

Let's say you create a few ground rules in your diary, and in any given day you allocate only two slots for meetings of one hour. When they're gone, they're gone. You then allow a further four for 30-minute meetings. You divide the rest of the day into 15-minute slots used for transit, personal work, or short informal meetings.

When someone calls you for an appointment, you need to do a little bit of diary triage. *"How long do you need? I have a 30-min gap available tomorrow, or if you need it I can give you an hour next week."* I'm going to bet that nine times out of ten people will take the half hour appointment. And, if they don't, you know that they feel that they really need that full hour. Just this question alone, with none of the aforementioned diary blocking, will cut down your meeting times by close to half, it will also impose a burden of brevity onto the person you are meeting with. This is all good as they will get you to the point quicker, and your meetings will be more effective and **you'll get *(literally)* heaps more done**.

[To be completely efficient, minimise the amount of people in the room, work under the basic premise that every extra bum in the chair adds 5-minutes to the meeting length – these 'extra bums' are exactly that (squatters), and usually superfluous.]

I find the most effective blocks to be the 15-minute ones. I use these primarily for internal meetings and I often schedule them two at a time. So let's say Donovan, one of Missing Link's big cheeses, wants to run an idea past me: he'll schedule 15-minutes in the morning, and a second 15-minute slot late in the afternoon. **Why?** Simply because in the first 15-minutes we'll grab a coffee and he'll take me through the idea; we'll discuss it and I may make some tweaks or have some suggestions. He will then work on this throughout the day and present it back to me later that afternoon. I see the changes, it's approved, and away we go. Initial and final approval - wrapped up in a quarter of the 'legacy' time.

Compare this to how it would work if we were like most corporations. Diaries are wrangled to make sure that all key-roleplayers can be in a room at one time. Donovan presents his idea, and there's much debate *(everyone has to have a chance to pee on the lamp post)*, discussion and opinion is bandied about and an hour later an action plan is agreed upon. Work gets done and, when complete, diaries are yet again wrangled - a meeting is set for two weeks Thursday. The first half of the meeting is spent recapping, the next part is spent presenting the tweaks, and the final bit is adding all the new tweaks that have risen over the period. Repeat as required. Ad infinitum *(or, at least it will feel like it)*.

It will take you two weeks to get an hour in the CIO's diary, but if you need 15-minutes, chances are you can get them today or tomorrow. Secretaries and PAs always look for blocks of an hour. And this needs to stop.

From now on, ask the thirty-today-or-sixty-next-week question for every meeting request you get - it'll change your life. Structure your diary better, make rules that everyone knows and be strict.
Better still, help other people structure their diaries better by not inviting them to meetings where they're not-critical, just because you don't want them to feel excluded. If you're worried about their feelings, buy them a Hallmark Card.
Managing your diary helps manage the time and productivity of ***every single person you meet****. It is an investment well worth making.*

LEGACY: YOUR JOB TITLE MEANS SOMETHING

Why? Because the business world we inherited was not necessarily a meritocracy. It was a militaristic hierarchy where "I'm the boss!" was used even when you weren't singing along to a Lonely Island song. Sadly, this is still too often the case.

Being an employer for around 18 years I've learnt a thing or two about promotions. It turns out that getting a new title does not in fact earn you the immediate respect of your peers and sub-ordinates, it simply gives you a new role to start living up to. To illustrate this, let me carry on the earlier name-dropping.

I had just come off a Midnight Oil tour and was flown straight to Durban to watch Whitney Houston arrive in all her glory *(that's two for the price of one right there).* The American management feared that they were coming to a backwater village and prepared as such. They brought washing machines *(obviously feeling the hand-washing method us Africans must employ was a bit slow)*, heaters, all foodstuffs, and to keep an eye on us, they brought 'Bill' our new crew boss.

Bill was a nice enough guy whose most amusing character flaw was getting his wallet nicked by hookers almost nightly. This happened to him *(for the first time)* the night he arrived and, to say the least, this unrelated incident immediately pushed him down a few notches on the ladder of respect *(but was pretty good for a laugh nonetheless)*. However, it was by lunch on the next day *(load-in day)* that his slipping-down-the-respect-ladder became a screaming plummet to the bottom.

Now, being part of a staging crew is pretty much an all-hands-on-deck affair. Everyone has their job to do, but everyone is also looking for ways to help others during their downtime. Well, almost everyone. You see, I don't remember Bill so much as raising a hand to help anyone, and he never once saw the inside of a truck and hardly ever the stage. Instead, he chose to attempt to delegate by two-way radio from the catering tent. It had taken the man less than 24 hours to lose all the respect of his team.

He was a stranger in a strange land yet, instead of trying to instill us with confidence, he sat back and let his team do all the work for him.

Bill first left catering after a few hours to answer a *(well bloody needed)* call of nature. Unfortunately, in a sad, inexplicable accident, the door to the porta-loo got jammed shut by about 10 lighting flight-cases. Also, his radio mysteriously stopped working, and thus the rest of us missed his cries of "Uuuhhhh, guys, I appear to be stuck in the porta-potty." It was 21h00 when we eventually let him out - apologising, and saying that we didn't notice him missing, what with us being hard at work and all. He got the message but was no longer considered by any of us to be the crew boss.

And that's the key here. Bill's fancy title wasn't worth the Access All Areas pass it was printed on. **Earning a title, it turns out, is not the hard** *(or even most important)* **part** - living up to it in the eyes of your peers and subordinates, is.

He went on to damage almost every piece of equipment he touched and I have enough 'Bill' anecdotes to last a lifetime, most involving prostitutes of various sizes, shapes, and in the case of the Cape Town show - genders *(but we'll leave it at that)*. Bill returned to L.A. three weeks later, never managing to recover from his early mistakes.

As a leader, it is important that your team respect you from word go - but that's your responsibility, not theirs. The mistakes you make early on can haunt you for a long, long time. See your new title as something you have to live up to, and not something that you own forever. You're not the Queen...

LEGACY: BUSINESS IS A SERIOUS AFFAIR

Why? Because, well, it was. The business world was exclusively run by serious old white men in old, dark suits.

As mentioned, I've sold presentations for a living for the past 18 years. People often ask me who our competition is. The answer is pretty simple - everyone with a copy of PowerPoint or Keynote *(or any of the other latest online presentation tools out there).* The reality is that any old idiot can put together a presentation. We're in business because so many do.

Lucky us.

The trick was realising that people that came to us were not actually looking for a presentation deck, **they were looking for a solution to boredom.** *(People were sick of being bored in presentations.)* Once this penny dropped, things changed rapidly. Sure we were a strategic consultancy, but we didn't have to act that way. We started laughing more in meetings, our working environment changed completely *(we have a treehouse, a fireman's pole and a shooting range)*, we started tattooing our staff and clients in our in-house tattoo studio, and the cash started rolling in.

If people wanted a solution to boredom, that's what I was gonna give 'em. And if we can make corporate presentations fun, then you can do it with your business - whatever it is.

Howard Mann *(mentioned earlier in FIRST AMONG EQUALS)* says that business is supposed to be fun to run. He's right, and it should also be fun for your staff and clients. The way to do this is to stop taking everything so seriously. I don't care what business you're in, your clients have a sense of humour. We've learnt this from brands like SouthWest, Nando's and even Washington Mutual.

"It's the nut-jobs that push the boundaries."

I haven't met a company yet that can't benefit from a little left-field thinking, and in every one of the truly awesome businesses I've worked with over the years, there's always been at least one loony that I wish worked for me, from insurance firms to merchant banks. They all have them. You see, it's the nut-jobs that push the boundaries; they see and think differently, and that's precisely what your business needs. Missing Link's strategic team believe *(and rightly so)* that when any group of smart people are struggling with an innovation-based problem, it's never because they're not smart enough, but always because they're too smart. What they need is perspective, and perspective comes free with the crazy brigade.

Apple said it best in their iconic television advert Here's to the Crazy Ones: **"... the people who are crazy enough to think they can change the world, are the ones who do."**

Think about it: companies already spend a fortune on agencies and the like, they do this ostensibly to buy marketing *(even when they have their own marketing departments)*. Actually though, what they are *trying* to buy **is a specific creative perspective**, and that creativity is a by-product of the craziness that is allowed to live *(and encouraged to thrive)* in these agencies. The good news is you don't need to outsource it. In fact, you shouldn't.

My challenge to you is this; the next person you interview, add 'craziness' as the attribute you want the most. Look, they still have to have all the right qualities you're looking for, I'm not asking you to replace one, simply to add another to the top of the list. I once hired a guy because he used to be a stunt man, and famed management guru Tom Peters tells how he once hired a consultant at the Business School at Stanford University based purely on the fact that he got into the Guinness Book of Records for baking a one-tonne cookie.

So if you want to change your world, make yourself a big warning label that says, "May contain nuts" and do whatever the hell you can to give yourself a reason to stick it on your front door.

I've made my living off being a little crazy. Look, it's not for everyone, but the way I see it **the people that are in the market for boring are spoilt for choice.**

ON BEING COMPELLING

LEGACY: BORING IS SAFE

Why? Well, boring is seen to be safe, because boring was in fact, safe. Is it still today? Seth Godin says that today, "Safe is risky", I'm inclined to believe him.

Okay, so I know I just went off on a tangent encouraging you to get a bit loopy, however what I really want is for you just to be boring-less. There isn't an industry out there that doesn't have the potential for this.

Hey, if the fuzz can do it, so can we. Take five minutes out of your day and check out the website of the Milwaukee Police Department www.milwaukeepolicenews.com. It's amazing. There's nothing boring about it, but the point I want to make here is that it's not wacky or crazy either.

Crazy is not the opposite of boring - compelling is. If you can't find anything compelling in your business, get a new job.

Years back I was in the market for a new car, someone recommended that I look at the Lexus Ls460. Boring right? Wrong. The experience I had was anything but that. From the crazy awesome test drive complete with blaring heavy metal, to the fact that Ricc Webb, the guy that sold me the car, hid three surprise gifts in the boot for when I got home - including a limited edition Vince Ray leather belt that said "Non-stop Rock 'n' Roll Voodoo Action". It wasn't branded, it was just rad. Ricc made Lexus compelling in so many ways. As cheesy as it sounds, it's the truth - I didn't just buy a car, I bought a story.

[D'ave here (the guy editing this book), with a quick adjunct: *after Rich grabbed his Lexus from Ricc, the power of the story alone moved me out of my Alfa and into a Lexus of my own. My experience? Equally awesome; and yet still completely unique (my gift was a sword!).]*

"Crazy is not the opposite of boring - compelling is."

A year later I persuaded Ricc to come work with us. I asked him one day about the fact that some would consider Lexus a boring brand yet my experience was anything but that. He replied to me like this, "Rich, there are no boring brands, just boring people delivering boring products. I just chose not to be that guy."

That's your job - don't be that guy, and make sure that your staff aren't either. I'm not saying that you need to get crazy (but give it a shot). Your job is to get interesting, and by that I mean interesting to me, your customer. Not interesting to you.

"...the people who are crazy enough to think they can change the world, are the ones who do."

Apple's "Here's to the crazy ones" advert. (1997)

LEGACY: YOU NEED TO THINK OUTSIDE THE BOX

Why? My granddad's generation started working at one company at 20 and retired from that company at 65. My dad started working in one industry at 18 and is still working in it at 67. That's a big box with high walls.

We've all heard it time and again: "Think outside the box - be creative!". The problem for most of us though, is that when we leave the box, we have no idea where we're supposed to go. Well, I think I have a plan.

For about two years now, my Twitter profile was simply, **"An Inked-ellectual gentleman"**.

Recently, I decided to add to it. To get inspired, I looked at what my friends wrote on their profiles. I wasn't.

There were tons of:

Thinker, writer, speaker.
Or entrepreneur, speaker, author.
The brave ones added in "father" or "husband", however almost everyone listed three things, and by and large all three of those belonged in the same box.

'Entrepreneur', 'speaker' and 'writer' all belong together. It's the entrepreneurial work that feeds the book, and it's the book that feeds the talk *(or vice versa)*. Whatever it is, it's all the same. How boring. No wonder you need to think outside your box.

I read a quote once that said, "If you need to think outside the box, maybe it's the box that needs fixing." I used to buy that, **I don't anymore**.

You don't need to think outside the box at all... you just need a heap more of them! My current Twitter profile reads as follows:

"A motorbike riding, boardgame playing, punk rocking, kung-fu fighting, kettlebell swinging, business running, microphone abusing inked-ellectual gentleman."

The only reason it wasn't longer is that I ran out of characters.

Running a business is certainly not what defines me. I am not an entrepreneur, any more than I am a biker, or a gamer. I am an entrepreneurial guy that plays games and rides motorbikes. Don't get me wrong, I'm obsessed with all of them. At one stage I had five businesses and read every book I could on the subject. Then I had 9 motorcycles. At the height of my kung-fu obsession I trained in martial arts 11 times a week. I currently own over four hundred board games and play at least one every day.

So what's my point?

It's basically this: It was kung-fu that got my anger and stress out from starting a business, and it's on my motorbike that I end up designing games. Playing games lets me consider different mechanics and strategies that I apply at work every day. Everything crosses over. I have a lot of boxes, and all of them are open.

So why is this important? Your brain is basically a series of intersections, and every memory you save creates a new crossroad. So, for example, if I was thinking about DHL the courier company, my brain would head off in search of relevant stored information. All of a sudden it would land at an extremely busy intersection, Coca-Cola Boulevard, and I would spurt out, "DHL is in more countries than Coca-Cola" a fact I remember from a presentation we made years back. DHL Drive, in my brain, intersects with Coca-Cola Boulevard. The more interesting and unexpected the intersections, the more likely you are to recall them, and more importantly, the more different your perspective will be from the guy next to you - and perspective is king.

That's the key here. Each one of my 'boxes' adds loads of little intersections. So, I find myself in a meeting struggling with a problem around resource management, instead of simply resorting to work-based examples from the work box, I may find myself drawing reference from Planet Steam in my board game box. And if I'm delivering a talk on Social Media, I may *(and did)* find myself referring to Ken Follett's WW1 work of fiction, Fall of Giants - thinking outside one box worked, because I had other boxes to rummage through.

I read a book once called Rules of the Red Rubber Ball. I can't say that I particularly loved the book, but I have never forgotten the quotation on the front page:

> *"The master in the art of living makes little distinction between his work and play, his mind and his body, his information and his recreation, his love and his religion. He hardly knows which is which. He simply pursues his vision of excellence at whatever he does, leaving others to decide whether he is working or playing. To him he's always doing both."*
>
> *James Michener*

I've not read much Michener, but he's my fucking hero. That right there is poetry, my friends. This obsession we have with boxing ourselves is terrible. You should never be able to use the term, "I am a ____er". Far better to say, "I am passionate about ______ing".

Look, I know we've all heard the term, jack of all trades, master of none, well there's some legacide right there. Unless you are a Japanese sword maker or a heart surgeon, you probably have a bit of wiggle room. The cool thing is that the more boxes you have, the better you become at all of them. 'Sum of the parts' kinda stuff.

Oh, and one more thing: For years, when people asked me what I was reading, I always answered with a work of fiction. I don't understand people that don't read fiction - it's alien to me. I've learnt more from the likes of Stephen Leather, Ken Follett and Bernard Cornwell than I have from any business guru.

Stop limiting yourself.

You are not the boxes that are your job, your hobby or your skill set. You are all of these and a whole lot more. If you live to work, you will regret it. No one cares. Search the entire world, and you will find but a small handful of statues built to businessmen, and most of those are because they did something else worthwhile.

Right now, head off to Twitter or scribble somewhere a new profile for yourself, make sure it covers a few real boxes and has more _ings than _ers. If you can't, buy yourself some board games or sign yourself up for kung-fu lessons. Whatever rocks your boat is fine, provided you're actually rocking it.

Now, speaking of boxes...

BOX YOURSELF

LEGACY: KEEP THE WORMS OUT

Why? The afterlife *(I'll explain)*.

I'm being fairly literal here and, while completely unrelated to business, I think that this example of legacide demonstrates the concept really well.

The idea of burial dates back over 130 000 years, although some scholars believe that it can be traced even further back to the Neanderthals.

In order to slow down the decomposition of the body, techniques such as embalming were introduced and, later, coffins. If you bought into the idea of, 'live fast, die young, and leave a good-looking corpse' then these coffins were for you. These low-tech boxes were used to protect the body from the bacteria that would attack it and cause it to decompose, becoming once again part of the ecosystem. If you're wondering why the ancients wanted their bodies preserved, it was simple - they needed a body for the afterlife - which is quite clearly ridiculous, and yet that's exactly what we still do. This is legacide at its most pronounced. Ask why people? **Why!?**

You see where I'm going with this yet?

We live in a 'green' world. A world where recycling is fast becoming the rule rather than the exception. We care about our planet, and we understand the importance of looking after it.

And yet we cut down trees to make boxes to keep out the bacteria that will turn us into nutricious fertiliser.

Really?

This is simply crazy. We should be burying ourselves in rapidly biodegradable cardboard coffins that contain agents that actually accelerate the decomposition process. *Would you like a dash of lime with that shroud, madam?*

We should have signs on the box inviting worms in for the Chef's Special.

"What about cremation?" I hear you say. Cremation is all well and good, but you're not really giving back to Mother Earth. If you decide to BBQ yourself though, for goodness sake, don't burn a tree with you. The idea that you get burnt in an oak coffin is criminal *(I also don't for one second believe that the funeral homes burn you in the coffin you paid R30k for, like they insist that they do, but that's another story altogether).*

Rent a coffin for the occasion if you really must. Or better still *(in both cases)* buy one from these guys: *legaci.de/creativecoffins.* You can even brand them. Love it. Oh, and their pay-off line rocks too: 'Green is the way to go'.

And if green really is your thing, you can become green. No, really. The Bios Urn will turn you into a tree. **How rad?**
legaci.de/urnbios

There is simply too much legacy here. Your family will go the traditional route unless you stipulate otherwise. So stipulate. Discuss it with them, and if you haven't already, discuss your thoughts on organ donation. What the world needs is one celebrity to hit the dark unknown in a cardboard coffin for it to become in vogue for the rest of us.

In the meantime though, you'll do.

PS. Look into Jae Rhim Lee's (decompi)culture - legaci.de/infinityburial

STEALTH BOMBERS & SUNK COSTS

LEGACY: FINISH WHAT YOU START

Why? No-one hands out medals to quitters. Except at SmokeEnders.

I remember when I was a kid and my teachers were always telling me that it's important to see things I do right through to the end. Get it done! And I get that, I really do. That said, blindly slogging on is certainly not always the most prudent course of action...

Let me explain. Let's say that you own a major aeronautics firm. You've spent 9 years and $9bn working on a $10bn/10 year stealth bomber project *(so you're 9/10th of the way there).*

With just one year to go, your Chief of Operations walks into your office and throws the latest edition of an industry magazine on your table - knocking over your skinny cappuccino. You open the mag and see that a competitor has just released a stealth bomber that can fly lower and faster than yours, and will be priced significantly cheaper. Dang...

So you're R9bn in and 90% of the way to completion - do you spend the last $1bn and hope for the best, or do you swallow the guaranteed $9bn loss and move on to the next project?

This is a tricky dilemma. Logic would suggest that we've spent so much time and money getting us this far that it would be crazy to just throw everything away, so we carry on. You see, as a nervous, tie-wearing, report-filing species we are inherently loss averse - so averse, in fact, that most people would slog on, and *hope* to regain some cash later, if any at all. **There's logic there**, but it's flawed. It's an issue of sunk costs.

Let me re-frame the problem for you:

Let's say you don't own the business. You've been approached by your former self asking for a $1bn investment to complete the project. Up until today's headline you thought it was a good deal, you hadn't invested in it before now, but think you could do well. Having just seen the headlines in the magazine, are you still willing to part with the $1bn?

Thought not.

We take our business personally. We get emotionally and mentally attached to it - and it clouds our judgement. We need to shift our perspective and look at things from the outside if we're to apply strictly rational thought. The big challenge is that we need to do it whether or not someone knocks over our coffee with a newspaper.

Measure your business projects constantly, but when you do it, try and put yourself on the outside. As it stands now, would you invest in project-x if you were an outsider? If you're anything like me, looking at your business from the outside will open your eyes in a way that will surprise you, and you'll see that, perhaps, some of the things you've been working on for a while need to be put to pasture.

LEGACY: HOOK 'EM WITH A GREAT PRICE

Why? Because everyone loves a bargain.

For years, Jo'burgers have travelled to work on the same motorway day in and day out. The Concrete Highway - as it has always been known - is a free-to-use freeway that loops around the entire city. Or at least it used to be...

You see, a few years back an initiative was set up by the government to introduce a toll-system to the road, where cars were logged whenever they passed under gantries, and then charged them accordingly.

Due to mass public outcry *(mine being one of the many voices)*, the system took forever to get up and running. They got it going eventually, but there was huge push-back from consumers, hardly anyone is even paying what they're billed and there are heaps of websites on how to get around the whole thing entirely.

However, as I was driving through a toll-booth just outside of Durban, this outrage suddenly struck me as a little odd. You see, here I simply handed the toll-booth attendant my credit card without so much as a second thought; toll roads aren't new to South Africans - we've been paying to travel on roads for years. **So, why the furore with the ones in Jo'burg?** Was it the high pricing? Yes, that probably had something to do with it, however I believe that it's something else. Quite simply I think our problem is that this road used to be free - and now it's not. *(Feel free to read up on cognitive dissonance in all its forms if you'd like some light reading on the topic.)*

In a study conducted by Anthony Doob back in 1969, mouthwash was used to demonstrate this behaviour. The examiners created a mouthwash - very similar in packaging and appearance to the current market leader - and launched it with an opening special that was around 35% cheaper than the competitor.

As you would expect, the difference had the product flying off the shelf.

They carried this on for a few months with similar results. When the special was over, and they reverted to their actual price of $0.39 - the same as the market leader - buying habits changed. **And changed fast...** You see people now mentally categorised this as a $0.25 value product, and not a $0.39 value product - so when the examiners changed the price, the consumer felt it was overpriced. The result: given the choice, consumers would revert to the market leader every time.

I believe that it is the exact same post-decisional dissonance *(again, look it up now and thank me later)* that is at play with the toll roads debacle. To South African drivers, the concrete highway was set at a price of 'free'. Changing that now is seen as an injustice. As taking something away.

I see this problem a lot these days, increasingly with businesses that are trying to build up a user base with launch pricing *(this typically occurs in the online arena)*. Rarely, if ever, have I seen it work. You can launch a freemium* version for sure *(like the guys at Evernote did so well)* where you give more value to a premium subscriber, however you'll find it hard to jump from free to a billed model. Of course, in most of these online businesses, if you aren't paying for the product or service, it's because you are the product - but that's another story altogether.

At the end of the day we're creatures of habit - we like things to fit in their pre-defined boxes and, when they don't, it creates internal angst that will often cause us to choose alternatives.

If you're starting out a new business, do your very best to bake your business model in at the get-go. It's a lot harder to get people to accept it if we try to change later. If you're already established and are thinking of completely changing your model or launching a new product at a discounted rate, understand the very real ramifications of what you're doing.

**Read Chris Anderson's great book FREE for more on pricing models.*
legaci.de/freethebook

ONE-TRICK PONY

LEGACY: YOU ARE YOUR PRODUCT

Why? People come to us to buy our products, or at least we think they do.

One of South Africa's most successful exports is the restaurant chain, Nando's. I'm a big fan of the brand, Robbie Brozin *(the dude that co-founded it),* and even the chicken. However if you held a gun to my head I'd have to admit to preferring the flavour of Mochachos, Yet Mochachos is nowhere near as successful as Nando's. Why's that? I expect it has something to do with a book Nando's wrote a while back called *It's Not Just About the Chicken*.

A few years back I was lucky enough to attend TED in Oxford. I'd recently bought and fallen in love with a Kindle *(Yes I have an iPad. No it's not a better reader. Yes I still carry a Kindle, and yes... you should buy one - more on this later)*. At one of the evening functions I found myself face to face with Amazon founder, Jeff Bezos. I commented on how much I loved my Kindle and asked him if he'd sign it for me. The dude grabbed the device, and with much enthusiasm and a big smile wrote, "Customers Rule - Jeff Bezos" across the upper right corner. I walked away grinning like a 14-year old at a Justin Bieber concert.

That night, Twitter was buzzing about how Amazon had just bought the on-line shoe behemoth *(you don't get to use that word nearly enough)*, Zappos. One of the tweets said, **"Jeff Bezos addresses the Zappos team"** It was a YouTube video clearly shot in Oxford. Curious, I watched it. Jeff gave a heartfelt welcome to the team explaining the whats and whys of the deal and how it would affect the Zappos crew. He spoke about the two companies and their shared passion for customer service. It was honest, believable, and I thought quite brilliant.

The next day at tea, I bumped into *(read: stalked)* Jeff again and asked him about the video. I told him that I own a presentation firm that often gets called on to make videos like these, yet it always takes loads of training to get such a slick message across, when his seemed so completely natural.

He smiled, put his hand on my shoulder *(OMG! OMG!)* and said, **"Do you remember what I wrote on your Kindle yesterday?"** I nodded. "Well," he continued, "I want to let you in on a little secret - **that's all I've got.** Amazon is a one-trick pony - and contrary to what people may think, the trick isn't books - it's making amazing customer experiences. I could have recorded that video last year, or two years from now, as could any one of my team, and the fundamentals would always be the same because it doesn't matter who we acquire, or which direction we head towards, our story will always be our story."

I looked at him and said, "Good thing it's a great trick." He beamed and replied, "Exactly!"

I got back to South Africa and took a long hard look at Missing Link. As I mentioned before, I realised early on that people weren't buying presentations from us, but were rather buying a solution to boring, and yet as we *grew up* we had started to believe all the presentation specialist PR we were getting. We started trying to sell better and better presos and were surprised that we were getting less and less thank you letters from our clients - even though our product had improved. You see people insisted on great presentations, that was a non-negotiable, but they were buying boredom-slaying experiences - **our one-trick pony**. As an important aside, it's also a shit-tonne easier to get staff excited about things like kick-ass customer experiences and boredom slaying, than the commodity we're actually selling.

So basically, Amazon's not about books, Missing Link's not about presentations and Nando's is not just about the chicken. Who knew?

You need to start realising that if you're anything like 99% of the market, your product may actually not be your differentiator, even when you think it is. And unless you're as good as Amazon, customer service probably isn't either. So what's left?

One client of ours, Anthony Nathan, stopped referring to his business as steel merchants and started referring to it as speed merchants. He went on to build an entire business around delivering the commodity faster than his competitors. And local bank FNB built an entire business around the principle of innovation. These are their kick-ass tricks, but what's yours?

Your trick here is to find your trick. *Take a piece of paper and draw a line down the middle, on the left list your products, and on the right list your differentiator, your "one trick". Be brutally honest, it's not about what you think, but rather what your customers would say (it's okay to ask them, even though they'll probably lie). Remember, and this bears repeating, you can tell yourself it is, but customer service is rarely a real differentiator - it's just part of what they pay you for.*

Sadly the truth is, if you're like many businesses, you may find yourself drawing a blank. That's okay, now you know. ***Just fix it.***

HELP WANTED. APPLY WITHIN

LEGACY: IF YOU WANT SOMETHING DONE, DO IT YOURSELF

Why? Because we have delusional self belief, and we're crap at delegating.

Speaking as an entrepreneur, when I started out I had to be all things for all people. I ran the company, I did the sales, I checked every slide and every video, I managed my calendar, I handled the interviews... you get the idea.

There were good reasons for this. The business was new, resources weren't what they are now and, really, it was only me who knew the **big picture** of what was going on.

That's certainly no longer the case. If you find yourself, years into the business, saying things like, **"If I want something done properly, I do it myself"** then you need to slap yourself up-side the head. You have only yourself to blame for the problems that come with those sentiments...

Sure, it could come down to your people, but you know what, you deserve the people you have. You hired them, and it's your job to pass your brains on to them.

So why don't we? Job security? Well, that's a really crap idea. It won't save your job and it will drive you insane.

There's a bigger problem here though, and that's ego. While we complain about how busy we are all the time, what we're *really* saying is, "Hey look at me, I'm smart and important and I'm constantly doing things."

It's time for that to stop. Your job from now on is to be embarrassed every time someone says to you, "How's things?" and your reply is, "Busy!". If that's your answer, you're losing at life. For some reason we see being busy as a status symbol, it's not.

So we need to strive to be **doing less stuff and thinking more**. It's the 'stuff' that you do that bogs you down. The thinking, on the other hand, will turn into cold, hard cash.

So, we need to free up your life and the only way to do that is to get help.

Step #1 is to teach people. You owe it to your own sanity to share as much of your knowledge as you can. Make sure they get it.

Step #2 is to trust people. Yeah, they'll mess things up a few times, but if you're not at risk of going out of business, let them make mistakes *(you did as well, if you remember correctly)*. If you have hired and trained the right people, they'll get it right soon enough.

Step #3 is to utilise people. For some reason many entrepreneurs, myself included, see having an assistant as a sign of douchebaggery. It really isn't. Every minute my assistant spends freeing up my time by planning a meeting or replying to a mail that I've let slip, is a minute she frees me up to work on things that are productive - like writing this. The stuff I'm good at.

If you manage your own diary and check your own mail: **stop**. *If you're frustrated at your people for not getting it, teach them better or replace them. And if you're saying you're busy, make very sure that it's doing something that is adding to your quality of life, and value to the business, and not detracting from them.*

ALL HAIL THE EX-RECEPTIONIST

LEGACY: YOU NEED A RECEPTIONIST

Why? Because you have a reception area. Why? Because your neighbour has one. Why? Because his neighbour has one. Why...?

This may seem a bit crazy, and even a minor detail, but that, as they say, is where the devil is...

Receptionists piss me off. No, really. Look, they serve a purpose - or, rather they could. They could do so much more than just take calls and make people sign a register *(one more legacy that needs to go - another time, perhaps)!* Here's a challenge for you: check out the 'recent items' list on your receptionist's computer - 10 million Zim dollars says that you will see Solitaire *(or Angry Birds on Google Chrome).*

I'm not suggesting that you fire your receptionist, I'm suggesting that you promote them.

Promote them to *concierge*, or *First Impressions Officer*.*

Then get rid of that shitty counter they sit behind. Unless you literally have a constant stream of people walking into your company, there's no reason that they should stay seated. When's the last time you greeted a visitor while sitting down? You don't, it's rude - and neither should they. Get them a nice regular desk, and suggest that they greet customers in front of it, with a handshake. I guarantee you that it will make an impression, which is kinda what they're there for, and your ex-receptionist will love it, too.

Then, empower them. Ask them to not just find out if your clients would like a coffee, ask them to find out how they like it, and remember it for next time. Tell them that their #1 priority is to make a good first, and last impression. I've freed up many people this way, and never cease to be amazed by the awesome stuff they come up with.

Oh, and if you really want to empower them, let go of the biggest legacy of all - your receptionist should answer all calls. That's a legacy from the time that we needed people to run a switchboard. At my companies, when the phone rings, whoever is free answers it - it really is that easy. If you must have a switchboard operator - outsource it. There is nothing worse for a prospective client than standing around waiting while your First Impressions Officer frantically fields calls.

Just do it. The immediate impact will be surprised and delighted clients. The longer impact will be the output of the conversations that those very clients have with their friends and co-workers. It's often said that people are your greatest asset, well then you should damn well make that asset work to its full potential. You'll have both happy clients, and a much happier receptionist if you do.

**A hat-tip here to Simon Woodroffe's must-read book "The Book of YO!"*
legaci.de/bookofyo

THE PROBLEM WITH THE WISE CROWDS

LEGACY: THE CROWD KNOWS BEST

Why? We grow up hearing that the 'whole is greater than the sum of the parts', and it usually is - just not when it comes to innovative ideas.

So, crowd-sourcing is all the rage. Let's see what the world wants, shall we? To do this, we can use Twitter, we can use Facebook, shit, we can use our company blog! It's all very exciting, but back to me *(I'm on a horse...)*.

I'm a big fan of James Surowiecki. He's the author of an excellent book on this topic called The Wisdom of Crowds but, in spite of the fact that I'm recommending that you read this, I think there's a bit of a flaw in this thinking when it comes to new ideas.

Here's the thing, and Henry Ford said it best years ago:

"If I asked my customers what they wanted, they would have said a faster horse."

Just because we have tools to aggregate the world, doesn't mean we have to listen to what they say... Usually you just get the most general answer. What you've done is created the world's biggest committee, and we know how effective committees are...

I was once at an innovation workshop in Geneva, run by a fairly large and well known firm that specialises in this kind of thing. It was pretty high-tech, and each of us was able to link our computers to central web-servers that were used to coalesce and process all the data. The software, to start, sounded pretty rad.

First we identified a problem that we wanted to solve on behalf of the workshop sponsor. Once we did this there was a general free-for-all where we all submitted ideas that could be used *(I even got the guys at the office back in*

SA to sneakily submit one or two) - all good so far. Then we married the ideas that could work together, and finally we voted on which we felt would work the best. And this is where the problem started...

A few of us were vocally pushing for some of the high risk ideas, however we did not seem to be swaying the crowd. Now you may think that this is democracy at its best, but I disagree whole-heartedly.

The famous Einstein quote goes:

"If at first the idea is not absurd, then there's no hope for it."

And of course, all the real cool and absurd ideas were completely killed off by the largely conservative *(as most crowds are)* group. In the end the three ideas we were stuck with were the three ideas that were the safest. They were tiny little step changes - the faster horses.

I left feeling disappointed and frustrated, and not in the least bit excited about the innovation we had created for the telecommunications client that sponsored the workshop.

You see, anytime you poll a large enough group, they will always aggregate to average.

"If I asked my customers what they wanted, they would have said a faster horse."

If your goal is to please everyone, by all means, put it out there. The crowd will work. It's your goal that's broken though.

Pleasing everyone = average. Average = boring. Boring = ignored...
...and ignored by the very crowd that you asked in the first place.

*I need you to understand that I'm not for a single second suggesting that you stop asking the crowd, I'm rather suggesting that you start using the information you get in a far more effective way. Generally speaking, when it comes to innovation, the people that you are asking are the very people that are looking to **you** for ideas. Like every worthwhile idea that has come before, you need to understand that at first it may make the market uncomfortable - and that's more than okay.*

*Spend less time asking the masses **if** they like your idea, and more time showing them **why** they will.*

ONE SIZE FITS ALL

LEGACY: WE KNOW OUR CUSTOMERS

Why? Well, we knew our customers, at least we thought we did. Of course, we used to think that the term 'customer' was a perfectly reasonable collective noun. One-size-fits-all and all that jazz.

Customer-centricity is a joke. Seriously, I don't even like the term, it's up there with best-of-breed and value-add. If you use it, ask someone near you to bitchslap you upside the head *(I'd do it myself, but I'm very busy, and likely very far away).*

Look, you need to understand, there are two reasons for my indignation. The first is that I hate buzzwords, they're like elevator music and logos on presentation slides - they're there, but no-one pays them any attention.

However, I have a bigger problem with the whole customer-centricity thing: **It doesn't work.**

Back in the day, I used to be quite the fan of Nokia. I had the 2110, 8810 *(the banana phone)*, the Communicator and, lastly, the E71 a few years ago. They were good, 'customer-centric' devices. Nokia did a great job of segmenting their base - they made a phone for gamers, a phone for business people, a phone for teens, etc. The problem was that I was a game-playing business man... That displeased the Fins at Nokia HQ immensely. How absurd they must have thought I was, daring to step outside their happy little box!

Nokia's strategy was simple - a different handset for everyone, at least a handset for all the main groups. This strategy did them well for years, until Apple's App Store ended the party. Basically, the app store did with software what Nokia was doing with hardware.

As much as I hate admitting it, that Steve Jobs guy wasn't a complete tosser. First, he developed the iPhone; not the world's most advanced smart phone, but the world's smartest *regular* phone, it was the quintessential horseless-carriage, "the everyman of smart phones" if you will. I remember arguing with people that it was crap and did so little compared to whatever fancy shmancy device I was using at the time. However, Joe Public bought it in droves.

Here's where Apple got really clever. They had created the sexiest **standard** *(or feature)* phone in the world, but it could do very little to help any specific group. So how were they going to get people with specific business/gaming/whatever needs to use it? They were gonna pass the buck.

On March 6, 2008, Apple released a developer API for the iPhone in the form of their SDK *(software development kit)*. Let the world solve the problem for them. And they did. Long-tail developers the world over gave the phone what they felt it needed, Apple simply made it easier for them. They did this by creating a standardised screen and button set up, allowing the developers to create just one app. This was in stark contrast to the trend at the time, which had developers creating multiple versions of their software for all the different phone models and button layouts. Then they had a centralised distribution centre *(the App Store)*, again, a huge step away from the completely decentralised sales strategy of the day.

What they did was ignore customer-centricity to focus rather on becoming developer-centric. Their end-goal was of course to be customer focused, but to do that they had to realise who they were really selling to - and that was the developers. Apple realised that they could never solve everyone's problems, so they let others do it for them. **Genius.**

The beauty of this approach is that it wasn't a generalised customer strategy, but rather one that allowed customers to build the exact functionality that they wanted and needed.

That's probably the real mistake here: grouping. In South Africa we refer to people by their LSM rating *(Living Standard Measurement - segmenting people by how much they earn and what they have access to)* a system built in the day when real-time data was unavailable. This is no longer the case, yet this legacy grouping remains.

We need to move from one-size-fits-all to tailor-made, and to get that right we need a re-think. Luckily, we have a whole plethora of new tools that can do just that.

So, is customer-centricity really that much of a joke? Only if you are using 'customer' as a collective noun. If you want to truly talk to me, get Richard-centric.

Take a pencil and paper and write down five attributes of your customer. Now get someone to phone a few of them and ask them to list five attributes about themselves. If you get one out of five you'll be lucky. Learning about our customers is easy, so is using that information to create a better product. The hard part is slaying the legacy of generalisation. But slay it you must.

THE SMELL OF OLD BOOKS

LEGACY: WORDS WORK BEST ON PAPER

Why? Because that's what we're used to. Books represent so much to so many of us, to mess with the formula in any way just feels wrong.

I'm a Kindle fan, a pretty big one in fact. I often describe my Kindle to people as being almost exactly like reading from an actual book... only better.

I'm forever being told, "Ah, but Richard, there's just something magical about holding a book in your hands, smelling the pages..."

If it's the smell of a book that intrigues you - you're doing it wrong. The magic of a book is in its words.

Sure, occasionally with certain books I like to have a physical copy on my shelf. However, for the most part, I'm all for the pixels. eBooks are more efficient, augmented, always the correct point size and easier to carry. Not to mention the fact that the text is searchable, you can highlight, see what others thought was important, and look up words like 'anomia' without having to find your dictionary.

Oh, and they don't involve a tree getting cut down - that's pretty cool too.

If you're reading a physical copy of this book, don't beat yourself up. I'd also want a keepsake. Know this though, it is because the Kindle is so wicked-cool that the printed version of this book is more than just words. There's pics, and colour, and scribbles. I wanted to compete so I had to bring something else to the party.

"The magic of a book is in its words."

For all the other plebs though, consider going digital, you'll thank me. So will trees everywhere. **Promise.**

AN IMPORTANT LIFE LESSON - FROM THE NICE PEOPLE AT CROCS

LEGACY: IT'S A SURPRISE - READ ON :)

So you're walking along one day and you see an antique oil lamp lying on the ground. No one's around so you figure "What the hell, I'll give it a wee rub" *(bet it's not the first time you've said that to yourself, eh?).*

Sure enough, out pops a genie. Before you get a chance to speak, he tells you that there's none of that three wish stuff happening today. He does however tell you that he has two surprises for you.

The first thing he does is click his fingers and tells you that you're 18 years old again. Your skin tightens, your bum lifts and, if you're a guy, those frustrating ear and nostril hairs find their way back to the places hair is meant to be.

He then clicks his fingers again and hands you a shiny new credit card. He goes on to explain that he has seen into the future, knows how long you're going to live *(a ripe-old age)*, and he has calculated how much you will spend on clothing throughout the rest of your life. He then tells you that he has put that **full amount** into the credit card and it's yours to spend on any clothing you want, and you **never have to pay him back**. Ever.

Good deal, right?

I ask this to audiences in my talks all the time and they always smile and nod. Of course it's a good deal.

However, he tells you, there's one wee condition at play here: You only have the next 4 years to use it. Once you turn 23, the card disappears and more importantly, you're **never allowed to buy clothes again**. You have to spend the rest of your life with the stuff you've bought already.

Still a good offer?

At this point my audiences start shaking their heads. I ask them why, and I get answers like:

• **Fashion changes** - what's cool now will not be cool next year *(just ask Glamour Magazine)*

• **We change.** We will not have the body of an 18-year old for ever.

Everything changes.

So no, we wouldn't take the deal. I mean, can you imagine you got the card in the midst of the Crocs phase*...? I can almost hear you saying, "Damn, these things are so comfy, and they'll never go out of fashion - let's stock up!".

And yet, this is exactly the behaviour we find acceptable when it comes to a far more important topic - education.

That's the Legacide here: We think education is something for the youth. This is a very dangerous mistake. Education, like fashion, requires a whole life of engagement.

So, where did this legacy come from? It came from a time when the job someone did when they left college/uni was the job they were still doing to some degree when they hit their retirement party. In this time, the things you learned in your twenties were mostly still relevant 30 years later - the world moved slowly.

For instance, my dad left school and studied to be a broadcast engineer. He went on to work at Scottish Television, then SABC and, now, at 67, he travels the world working on most of the biggest sporting events as, you guessed it, a broadcast engineer. His education was the foundation that his entire career was built on.

Would this still be the case if my dad was 20 *now?*

Consider this: a 23-year old that came for an interview with us last year - this guy looked me straight in the eye and explained that he'd been doing social media for three years now, and really feels that it was time to explore something new. After just *three years!* WTF?!

What's even more important to note here is that the job he was an 'expert' in, didn't even exist 10 years ago, and almost certainly the job he'll be bored of 10 years from now, doesn't exist today.

Is the 23 year-old wrong? Who knows, that's not for me to judge. However it does illustrate the challenge facing the construct of education as we know it. We need to move from the foundational learning of days gone by, to a more perpetual learning style that will suit the modern workplace. Life long learning is critical!

There's more to this story than that, though... The average age of retrenchment in South Africa is 40 and above and I imagine it's not so different elsewhere in the world. Why is this happening? Why are we putting all the company wisdom out to pasture? **There are three main factors here:**

Factor #1 is exactly what we just discussed. In many environments, the world-of-work is a vastly different place when you're 40 compared to when you were 23. *The material you studied so intensely at university is simply, for the most part, no longer relevant.* You're out of date, bub.

Factor #2 is that companies are a bit like commercial travel - there are far fewer spaces in the good seats up front.

Your career is a game of musical chairs, every year someone takes a chair away, and only a few are left with a desk to sit behind. You're one of many.

Factor #3 is the fact that your salary has been compounding year-on-year *(my mate Steve Liptz calls compounding the 8th Wonder of the World).* This means that a 40-year-old mid-level manager could be earning almost twice the salary of a 30-year-old peer, and that 30-year-old is still unattached and more than willing to work nights and weekends. You're overvalued.

Now ask yourself: who do you think will get cut when times get tough?

This story gets even scarier as you look further into it though.

Let's say my dad was one of the unlucky ones that found himself retrenched at 40. How would that impact on our family? Turns out, not so badly. Both my sisters would have been finished high-school, one was working already, and I would have had just a few years to go. My family would have struggled, but we'd have been okay.

Let's look at my generation, though. Getting married at 20 and popping a few children out would be deemed a big mistake. Far better to wait until your early- to mid-thirties when you can afford it *(and them)*, right?

[By the way, this is a complete crock in and of itself...

At whatever life stage you find yourself pregnant, you make it work. Even the 16-year olds. I'm not saying that I advise it, however, I will say that it certainly isn't the life sentence people say it is. Your kids will be out of school before you reach your forties. What a win!

Today's logic is utterly flawed. We selfishly hang on to our youth as if it's the only age we're able to enjoy ourselves. My parents have been travelling the world, going on long holidays since I left school - and at that point in their life they were able to do it in style, no back-pack was carried and no hostel visited *(as I write this, my folks are at the World Cup, in Brazil after two, curry-licious months in India).*

Done with that. As you were.]

"We think education is something for the youth. This is a very dangerous mistake."

If one of my peers find themselves retrenched at 40, it will be an entirely different story. They will have one child in primary school, one in nappies, and a third on the way - they will certainly not be okay.

So what does this have to do with education? Well, what if the person that had the most experience also had the latest, most relevant knowledge? That person would be a very real asset, and more importantly, if that person did find themselves out of work, they'd be a lot more likely to find work again.

So what's the plan here? Well I think this is a big problem that needs a big solution. Many radical educators are calling for the death of the big tertiary institutions. I believe that we're more likely to win this one if we get these institutions to change to a new *(more profitable)* business model.

Imagine if Harvard gave out a degree in a third of the time, but it had an expiry date. Imagine you had to study two weeks a year - in any field - to keep your original degree active.

Remember, the degree as it stands now isn't for you anyway, it is to make the job of the HR manager at the FIRST job you get, easier. The first job! As it stands now, that's all that matters. Seriously, I do not think that I have belaboured this point enough. The four years you spent studying that degree that your parents told you that you **absolutely needed** *(and sadly, you probably do if you plan to work in a large corporation, which is, for the most part, a really crappy idea)* will be an important factor in landing you *one* job only - thereafter, people care about experience, references and track record. There are obvious exceptions, but you get my point.

The next chapter is a good example of this.

Change the game! *Educate yourself to get a better position in the company you're in, and use that position to get a better job elsewhere. And if you're an educator, change the game, too. Sell expiring degrees that rely on life-long top-ups. Great for you, and great for brains everywhere.*

Knowledge is not certification, it's a beautiful thing that you need to be doing ***daily*** *to stay relevant. Oh, and I mean in-depth knowledge, not the inch-deep / mile-wide education you're lying to yourself about by clicking links on Twitter. The last thing you want is to be the only guy in the room still defending the comfort and practicality of your silly rubber shoes.*

**As an aside, I recently bought a pair of Crocs. They look like boating shoes; navy and white. The thing is, as much as I loved the shoes, it took me a month to convince myself that it was okay to buy them. Sure, they looked nothing like the originals - still, they're, well, Crocs. This reluctance goes to show you the power of legacy when it comes to brands. I decided to practice what I preach, I was going to be the bigger man. I was going to show society that I would not be judged. To hell with your opinions, I'm a grown man, if I want to wear a pair of Crocs, I damn well will. So I bought them...*

*...an hour later I caved in and cut off the "Crocs" label. Baby steps *shrugs**

LEGACY: THE BEST ROUTE TO YOUR DREAM JOB IS THROUGH UNIVERSITY

Why? We assume that all employers have the same lazy hiring criteria as the HR teams in large corporations, but the truth is, many don't.

My sister wanted a job in travel. Free flights; who wouldn't? So off she went and studied it. The course was a year long, her career in travel lasted a month. Apparently, no amount of free travel was worth it for her.

My sister is one of the lucky ones though, she only invested a year in studying for this non-starting career, you know, because it was "the right thing to do", but many of my friends spent 4 years at uni, and another few in a job they hated, before they eventually found something they really liked. Now that's a waste. What we really need is a try-before-you-buy system of sorts, and on that, back to my sister...

She found herself needing work. Fast. While deciding what she wanted to do, she found a job as an assistant at an architecture firm. This guy was no ordinary architect, though. He was the designer of houses and pads for the rich and famous. Super-high-luxury ridiculously expensive living.

Well, as it happens, working there made my sister realise that she really liked this field, so she asked if she could help with draughting. He said yes and sent her on a three month evening course. Within six months she was a full-time draughtsman / woman / tron / wtf?!

Fast forward a few years and my sister had her own firm. Like her boss before her *(not an actual architect)*, she was a designer of buildings that only needed an actual architect to rubber stamp plans for a small fee before submitting them to council. Within two years she was one of the most prolific designers in her region. And within ten years she wrote an exam that allowed her to, with no further education and on the back of her experience alone, design buildings up to 10 storeys high without the need for anyone else's 'rubber stamp' - and my sister has no inclination to build 11 storeys.

All this happened in the time it would take a traditional architectural student to study, get their degree and finally enter the workforce for the first time. My sister has a head start on them that only the very, very few would be able to catch. **Compounded experience, ability, and attitude, trumps the degree.** Of course, in large corporations you wouldn't get in, in the first place, without the paper, but really, large corporations, how boring.

I see this in my own *(albeit entrepreneurial)* business all the time. The easiest way to get a senior position in our company is to have a job here. This sounds silly, but let me explain. Once you're in, you have the chance to shine and, if you do actually shine, you'll find that we'll do everything we can to help you attain any position you desire. My old business partner started out as a production assistant, and our general manager started off as concierge.

So, what am I saying here? *Don't get your kids to study at all? No! Just do your best to make sure that they have experience in a field before they set out to study it. Almost every firm I know has internship programmes, and most companies, including my own will happily allow people to pop in and job shadow (no, the three days they did in Grade 10 won't cut it). Surely when it comes to a decision of this magnitude, we should let our kids try before they buy.*

BEST-PRACTICE DOESN'T MAKE PERFECT

LEGACY: BEST-PRACTICE

Why? Sadly, it's just too easy to go with the flow. We assume if everyone's doing it well then it must be right. You know, like lemmings.

One thing that always confuses me is the acknowledgements section at the beginning of books. Everyone skips over them. Everyone. My Kindle even does this for me. And yet there they are, in every book.

There has to be a better way. Let's take this book, for example. Now, I would obviously like to thank **Don Packett**, my friend and business partner for helping me read the drafts and more importantly always giving me shit for not finishing it. And, of course, I'd want to thank the uber-talented **Wonderland/ Works** for all their great illustrations, and **Jackie Scala** for the amazing layout and design work. Then of course if I didn't thank **D'ave Meyer,** founder of Year Zero, for editing this and getting it to make sense I'd be a fool - partially because I may need his help again in the future, but mostly because he's a rad guy, but also kinda sensitive.

[**D'ave edit:** Mostly because, if he didn't, I would have filled it in my damn self. And he did leave out 'Hawking-ly intelligent']

And there you go. You just read the acknowledgements. However, if I'd slapped them at the beginning they would be lost. No-one would know I'd thanked them *(probably not even them).*

Look, I get that no-one actually needs to read the acknowledgments - that's not the point. The point is that just because it's 'best-practice' *(ie - everyone does it)*, doesn't mean you have to stick to it. In fact, if you want to stand-out at all, you need to defy convention every chance you get.

So I put the thank-yous in the middle. Hell, I could even squeeze in a few more, I could thank my wife, **Jasmine**, for all the crazy hot lovin', and **Calumn** and **Bailey** - my kids - for the never ending stream of rad they bring to my life.

I've put these right bang-smack in the meaty parts of this book, and you read them. **Convention be damned.**

'Best-practice' is everywhere - it's in your business cards, your hold-music, and in the crappy, crappy gifts you send clients every Christmas. Seriously, what's that about? You are sending gifts at the very same time that every single other supplier is doing the same - your gift is a lovely leaf, that's on a forest floor, in autumn. What's even worse is that you're putting your name on the leaf *(or gift)*. Stop it. If it has your name on it, it's not a present, it's an advert. No one wants to pull out a fancy pen in a meeting that was clearly given for free, nor do any of us have any desire to be marketing tools for you. The same goes for the branded clothing you keep giving your staff. That said, I guess you can never have enough shirts to paint the house in...

I've made it mandatory that any gifts sent from Missing Link to clients are never branded, and they're certainly not sent out at Christmas. We sing our own hold-music. Our business cards are cheeky and collectible. As every-one does 'good' coffee these days, we've invented our own way to serve hot chocolate - I highly recommend that you try the 'Squirrel Shit'. We look at anything that's expected and try our best to change it - and our clients and prospects love us for it. On that note, I'd like to thank **Samantha**, a lady who for 10-years had to put up with, improve, and execute brilliantly every hare-brained idea I had *(well, not quite every - she was way too smart for that).*

Miss you Sammo

In every company, in every town, and on every street, there are hundreds of examples of best-practice. It's changing these that make standing out so easy for us. If you remember just one thing from this book it's this: stop accepting things at face value. **Reclaim yourself - question everything.**

That's your job here. Challenge convention and change the mundane! It's everywhere - we spend so much time trying to stand out with the big things, and not nearly enough time differentiating the details. The best thing about the wee details is that you get the chance to change them ten times a day. The big hitters are far more occasional. Do this, and I promise you it won't just be me doing the thank-yous.

P.S. Mum, Dad, Shiv, Va - love you guys.

LEGACY: THE COLOUR OF YOUR CREDIT CARD CORRELATES TO YOUR WEALTH

Why? Read on a bit...

So when I was younger, if my dad wanted to show off, he'd simply flash some wallet-gold and people would look him deep in the eyes, pound their fist to their heart, and mouth the word, "Respect". Basically, there was a direct correlation between the colour of your credit card and your wealth, ergo willy size, i.e. guys with gold cards got laid a lot more than the rest of us *(of course I was about 16 at the time and wasn't getting laid at all, however I do feel I made up for that in my creative and frequent masturbatory antics).*

The reason for the colour differences was simple: The colour of your card *(blue, gold, black, etc.)* was directly related to the amount of pre-approval your card had. Remember, in those days we had those big-ass credit card machines that would take an imprint of your card on a piece of carbon paper by ripping a plastic roller thing back and forth with a fair amount of elbow grease, then manually filling out an amount.

The colour of the card simply told the vendor how much credit the bank felt that you were "good for", so that they didn't hand out 34" tube TVs to just anyone. It was an elegant solution to pre-approval. Fast forward a few years, and we now have credit card machines capable of checking our balances in seconds, yet we still hang on to this legacy, albeit for ego value.

A while back we were running an Innovation Lab for one of the banks, and one suggestion was to allow the client to customise their plastic card. "Oh, no," they said, "Card Division would never allow that - it would clash with our colour-coding system."

Here's the thing: In the beginning there was a problem *(managing credit limits)* and a smart person somewhere came up with a beautifully elegant solution *(colour coding)*. Years later, the initial problem disappeared *(connected credit card terminals)* but we're stuck embracing the outdated solution. Now, you could argue that this is just a small detail, and its purpose has evolved to now more of an ego play anyway. You'd even be right, but you need to start somewhere.

While this is quite obviously a straight-up case of falling into the solution-trap, there's more to it than that. It's Legacide on a smaller scale, but it has a big effect. It's not enough to look at your core products, you need to look into the detail too. Legacide exists everywhere, and when you sweat the small stuff, it will pave the way for you to change the big stuff too.

Take a magnifying glass to your business. Look at some of the seemingly arbitrary practices. Why do we start work the time we do? Why do we use a specific piece of software? Get a notepad and question the next five things that you come across. The smaller the better. Fixing the arbitrary problems helps to create a culture in which Legacide is hunted, and eradicated.

LEGACY: YOU HAVE TO KNOW YOUR AUDIENCE

Why? I believe this is perhaps a mis-interpretation as opposed to a true legacy, however we have carried and repeated this mis-interpretation for years.

I'd be remiss if I was to write a business book without having at least one token presentation section - so here it is! Search any list of presentation tips, and "know your audience" is almost certainly going to make an appearance, and yet it is this tip that, more than almost any other, leads to boring presentations.

As has been mentioned, I've owned a presentation firm for 18-years. However, I have also been a professional speaker for around 10-years. My market has almost always been large corporations of business professionals, which is kinda strange given that I'm an ex-roadie with a dodgy haircut, a potty mouth, and more tattoos than you can shake a hat at.

However, none of these are secrets, people still hire me, then ask me to understand that their audience is fairly conservative and request that I, "tone things down a bit."

Now customer service is extremely important to me so I nod thoughtfully, look my client straight in their eyes and explain that this will be no problem whatsoever.

Which, of course, is complete and utter bullshit.

Why do I do this? Well in fairness if you want to hear your pet "miaow", you probably shouldn't have bought a dog. That aside though, is it because I'm convinced that I know more about their audience than they do? No, not really.

Bear with me for a sec here. Making a speaker believe that their audience is boring is actually quite dangerous advice. You see for a presentation to be effective, it must be engaging, and generally speaking, being bland and uninspired, isn't.

Also, an audience is not a one-size-fits-all collective. **They are individuals.** They have their own thoughts and opinions. That guy in the front row in the power-suit could well be wearing women's underwear, and the lady in the middle could be both an accountant and a cage fighter *(seriously)*. Also, if you're speaking to a group of big business professionals, you can pretty much guarantee that many of them went to university and, based on that, you can pretty much guarantee that many of them had crazy parties, and got crazy wasted. I say 'pretty much', because you have no real idea, however it's fair to say that 90% of the people in 90% of your standard audiences, can get through films like The Hangover without dying of shock - in fact, most of them probably even laughed a little *(a lot)*.

The only thing you can know for sure about an audience member is that they all come pre-equipped with finely tuned authenticity detectors. The first sign you give them that you are not authentic, the credibility of your message goes out the window, also their enjoyment of the overall experience is diminished.

So that's why I stick with being myself. When you're on a stage, you want to be the best at something. And you can be. I am 100% of the time, the single best version of myself in any given room - as are you. People pick up when you're being yourself and, provided you're not a complete asshole, they'll generally like you for it.

It is also far easier to bring an audience to your wavelength than it is to try and guess what theirs is.

Using the afore-mentioned film, let me give you an example of how I've opened a perceived "conservative" audience.

"Hey everyone, my name's Richard Mulholland and I look forward to spending the next 45-minutes with you. Before we kick off though, the organisers warned me that y'all are auditors and thus probably boring and conservative. So I just thought I'd do a wee test for myself.

Right, hands up anyone here that didn't see The Hangover [a small smattering of hands]. Now, those of you that saw it, hands up how many of you died from shock while watching it [laughs]. No? Good! Then I can absolutely guarantee you that you'll make it out of here alive today, as there's nothing I could possibly say to you that will be even close to as shocking as seeing that Asian guy's junk - and I don't mean his boat [more laughing]. So if you keep all that in mind, we're gonna be juuuust fine."*

The audience is now tuned to my wavelength, so I'm good to go.

Oh, but listen, before you start F-bombing a group of nuns, use common sense. I certainly pick which bombs I drop to which crowds. I just do this with information I learn about the audience **during** the talk, and not before it. I also personally don't mind losing a small percentage of people - you can not and should not be trying to please everyone *(with your delivery or your content)*, which will put you in the safe zone, and when it comes to presentations, safe is painfully boring, and boring is painfully ineffective.

What you do need to understand, and this is where the legacy mis-interpretation comes in, is that 'Know your audience' is important from a content point-of-view. In other words, *know what they want to get out* of this presentation.

Understanding the context and mindset of your audience is critical for structuring your message to add the most value. It should go without saying that your job as a presenter should be to add more value to your audience than you should be taking - yes, even *(especially)* when you're selling.

I recently saw a guy stand up in front of a group of first year university finance students and thinking of them as 'kids', spoke to them as if they had just entered high-school. He lost *(and insulted)* them in seconds. He would have been far better off had he considered that this was an event structured around thought leadership *(the reason they attended)*, instead of just thinking of them as 'young'. **Understanding context is crucial.**

*For me, a better phrase would be, **'know your event'**. There's a reason those 500 people are sitting in front of you and if you can understand the success criteria for the event, then you have a far better chance of pitching your message to win for everyone. You need to be brutal here mind you, ask yourself constantly, "Will saying **Y** help me deliver on the objective of event **X**?". If the answer's no, scrap it.*

And if you are an event organiser, your time would be far better spent explaining the event's success criteria than it would be making assumptions about people's possible sense of humour - or lack thereof.

*Top tip: Anytime at all that you are polling an audience using the 'raise your hand' method, always make sure that the answer you want the most involves them keeping their hands down. No one really wants to raise their hand, so use this to your advantage, it's a great way to win the vote of the fence-sitters and indifferents.

THE GOOD KINDA LEGACY

LEGACY: BUSINESS SUCCESS IS MEASURED IN DOLLAR SIGNS

Why? Go back 20 years and the only way you were going to be able to show your peers how successful you were was with the car you drove and the house you lived in. Today though, you have options.

Of all the sections I've written so far, this will be the one that is the most personal, so if the idea of me literally soul-searching one keytap at a time is too much for you, feel free to jump on ahead.

If you decided to stay, best you pass me a tissue - I'm feeling a wee bit emotional.

At the time of writing this chapter, I was facing a really big challenge. I had been in negotiations for close to 6 months with a company that was looking at buying Missing Link. The numbers we were looking at were somewhere between R10m and R15m *(to put that in context, that was enough to wipe all my debts, buy a small mansion, a snowboard apartment in Austria, a garage full of motorbikes, and still have some capital left over for my next venture).*

Yet, I also considered going a completely different route altogether: I considered walking away from the deal, and selling 30% of the business to Sam *(the managing director at the time)* for R100 - enough to buy me a Starbucks latte. This would allow me to lose a lot of the day-to-day stress, while still being part of the fun stuff.

I liked this idea, it felt right to me *(even if my bank manager disagreed).* So why was I apprehensive? Surprisingly, it wasn't about the money *(at least it's not what the money could buy),* but rather my ego. Like any entrepreneur, I wanted to be seen as successful - I craved it. If I went ahead with the 'Sam-Plan' I'd probably not be able to add to the collection of motorbikes *(okay, so for this one I made a plan),* and would certainly not be getting the holiday house in Zell, and this bothered me immensely. It felt like admitting that I was a failure...

But then, as I was riding to the airport one day, screaming at the top of my lungs to Pennywise, it struck me: all I had to do was re-define what success meant to me. You see, some measure success on what you've made, others on what you've done. The epiphany for me was that I wanted to jump the curve from the former to the latter. A month later, Sam gave me R100 for 30% of Missing Link*.

Turns out I wasn't alone in this thinking.

I'd like to tell you the story of one of the most inspiring and successful people I've ever met. His name is Taddy Blecher and he is the founder of both the CIDA City Campus - an inner-city university in Johannesburg, South Africa - and the Maharishi Institute.

Taddy started out his career as a 6-figure-actuary working for some of the biggest and best consulting firms in the world *(he won 'Consultant of the Year' three years in a row at Monitor)*. However, based in South Africa he felt that he was reaching a ceiling of sorts, so he decided to go international. Also, like many South Africans, he was increasingly worried about the rising crime situation.

He sold off his considerable assets and sent out his CV - and the phone started ringing, "Would you fly to Sydney for an interview with Firm X?", "Can you pop out to New York for an interview with Firm Y?" The sky was the limit - he was all set to pick and choose whatever job he wanted. And then he stopped...

He looked at South Africa and realised that he didn't in fact want to leave the country of his birth, he just strived to grow. He'd been chasing that growth in terms of his career and wealth, but he could chase it elsewhere, too. This is when he started playing with the idea of higher education for previously disadvantaged individuals that wouldn't otherwise have the chance - to make SA a better place, rather than just padding his wallet. He realised that instead of running from SA's crime, he could actually use education to do something about it.

Overnight, his passion changed - he negotiated the use of an abandoned building and roped as many friends in as he could. He knew that he needed to teach subjects like Computer Science - but they couldn't afford computers. So he took an old computer keyboard, went to the nearest photocopy shop, and ran off as many copies as he had students so they had a head-start in learning to type. And so it began...

Slowly but surely, **he started a movement**. He created a free university that educated hundreds of young adults, these young adults literally ran the place. They built desks, made meals *(every student gets a free vegetarian lunch every day)*, cleaned up, tutored, and even ran extra-mural classes such as karate and Transcendental Meditation.

His students went on to win local computer competitions *(just stop and consider that for a second - they learnt to type on a photocopied keyboard)* and, more importantly, they started graduating. To date, CIDA has had thousands of students pass through their doors, but the reach has been far larger than this - entire families have been transformed. And the world has noticed *(he won the WEF's Global Leader for Tomorrow Award in '02).*

CIDA is supported by firms like Investec and Dell, its patrons include Oprah and Branson, and Taddy himself has spent time on Necker Island with the likes of Larry, Sergei, and Jeff Bezos. He may not be living in a mansion anymore, but I challenge anyone in the world to say that he is not one of the 10 most successful people they have ever heard of.

Most of us try to change a balance sheet, Taddy's changing the world.

"...success is simply a state of mind."

That's the kind of success that I want, and work towards. More importantly, that's the legacy I want to leave behind. You see there's certainly some legacy that's good - it's that thing you're remembered for (*at least, you hope it will be good*). If you asked me what success meant to me, I'd say that I'd like to be mentioned on the same page in the history books as Taddy is. This is partly what led to the co-creation of the social-entrepreneurship company I started with my mates Jason and Adrian, HumanWrit.es, in which we're trying to save the world, one wee square notebook at a time.

So what has this got to do with you?

Ask yourself why you're doing ***'all of this'****? Ask what will be the best story to tell your grandchildren. If you're anything at all like me, it won't be how many millions you've made yourself, but how many millions you've helped others make. The good news is this:* ***success is simply a state of mind*** *- and you can change your mind whenever you feel like it.*

* I recently bought this shareholding back for quite a bit more than the R100. The irony is that Sam sold her shares back to me for exactly the same reason that I sold them to her in the first place. Her success parameters shifted. Personally I find this to be quite beautifully poetic - albeit expensive.

WHY AND WHY NOT

LEGACY: ONWARDS AND UPWARDS!

Why? Progress is about moving forward, so that's where I'll look for my innovation.

Growing up, I remember my cousin Robbie telling me what I imagine to be an urban legend about a group of university students that were given a philosophy essay to write. The topic was "Why?".

Many waxed lyrical with wordy essays on the deep 'existentialism of blah blah' or the 'self-evidence of this and that', but only one student received a distinction. His essay was just two words long:

"Why not?"

He got an A+, but I want to find him and punch him in the nose.

'Why not?' is simply not a good enough answer! Before I head into the last wee chapter, I want to summarise the essence of this book.

'Why not?' is quite frankly a cop out. Yes it's quirky and has a creative, 'let's head to the great unknown' feel about it. 'Why not?' is exciting, and cool, and needed! But it is definitely step #2. Step #1, the most crucial step in all innovation - is to ask 'why?'.

You see in our experience, the reason most people *(ourselves included)* are not more innovative is because they are stuck in the past *(the "why?" stuff)*, and not because they are scared of the future *(the "why not?" stuff)*.

So, first ask **why,** then only, ask ***why* not**.

I hope I've got you thinking about legacies that exist in your business; in everything from product development, to 'being the best' to marketing. I would like it if you re-thought personal things like success... and your funeral.

Most of all though, I hope that I have instilled in you the need for **retrospective curiosity**. I, personally, find myself asking "Why?" every day, for any number of things. "Why is *this* okay, when *that* isn't?", "Why was this company successful *then*, but not *now*?", "Why did that idea fail *then*, but work *now*?"

What changed, and more importantly, what didn't? I think the key to business survival is somewhat Darwinian. We need to ask why we have that, or why we do this, and we need to ask it constantly. If it's no longer relevant, we need to kill it off.

Survival of the fittest indeed.

The idiom goes: ***Curiosity killed the cat.*** *Well, to hell with the cat, it has nine lives. You don't though, so you need to get curious, and start asking "why?" a whole heap, and you need to start now. I've said it before and I'll say it one more time - hell I even have it tattooed on my left bicep:*

Reclaim yourself. Question everything!

"Reclaim yourself. Question everything."

LEGACY: BUSINESS BOOKS SHOULD BE AROUND 350 PAGES LONG

Why? Patience buddy, I'm getting there.

Business books are too long by half *(more than half actually)*. For the most part you get what the author is saying in the first two chapters, and the rest of the book is simply filled with fluff and case studies. The book you're holding right now is a stellar example of this...

I've been explaining the Legacide concept to people for years. It takes me approximately 5-mins in a talk to get the idea across, and yet here you are, around an hour and fifty minutes in and you're only just reaching the end. **Why?**

This is how I see it: the average novel *(story, not business)* runs at around 350 pages. It's the amount of time it takes for an author to set the scene, build the plot, and close the loop; while still maintaining a degree of excitement. *(budding authors, check out Ken Follett's free masterclass on the importance of pacing* - legaci.de/kenfollettmasterclass)

Now, as a huge fiction fan, if a book is structured and paced well, I'll devour every last page. Hell, if the story calls for it I'll read two or three times the amount of pages. **You see fiction is a leisure.** The longer I can relax with a good book, the more value it has given me. But this thinking has a side-effect.

Do me a quick favour: using your thumb and forefinger show me *(or the person next to you)* how thick a book should be. My guess is that the gap is about an inch *(I hate myself for not going metric here - bloody legacies)*. Right? That's what those novels have done - they've taught us how thick a book should be...

...and that's why we struggle to finish so many business books we start reading *(and why services like Get Abstract or Blinkist are so popular)*. Because we think that's how thick books should be. But you see business books scratch a different itch. They're not leisure, they're learning. The faster I can consume your knowledge, the quicker I can consume someone else's.

(check out: legaci.de/whybizbookssuck*)*

However, that doesn't work for the publishing industry... Publishers want us to create books of a similar size, because they look right on the shelf. **That makes no sense to me - all books are not created equal, so why are they created a similar length?** To quote a friend of mine, Patrick Kayton *(the founder of Cognician.com)*, "You can see the part in every business book where the author gets bored". Truer words were never spoken. If I'm to be completely honest with you, as I type this, I've written 14 of the chapterettes that make up this book, and I know that I need to double that, but I'm already worried that I've already said too much *(sorry, I know this may seem confusing as my intention is that this is the last chapter, but hey - linear shminear)*.

In today's day and age, the *width* of a book is simply no longer a factor. Why? Because width has no bearing when you're buying a book for a Kindle *(iPad/iRiver/eBook/wHatever)*. What *does* have bearing is *time*. Like I said, business books are **work**, or at least work-related. Get in, get the point, move on. Even if you're loving the read, there are other things to do, and other books to get through.

And if you think you're getting bang for your buck with a big book, think again.

Let's say you just paid $9.99 for this book *(Book A)*, and $9.99 for another business book that's twice the length *(Book B)*. Some would say that Book B offered you twice the value for money. **Me, I'm calling bullshit on that.** The time it takes a business person to read the extra hundred or so pages is worth far more than the $5.00 they have 'lost', especially considering the fact that they don't really get any additional content from those last 100 pages.

It's kinda like a TED talk: it takes a lot of work to distil a one hour lecture into just 18-minutes. The distillation process takes time - that's the speaker's challenge - and it's also why TED talks are so good. The distillation forces them to be better. They're distilled to their **knowledge-concentrate**.

Well you know what? It's the author's challenge too. If you're writing something these days, the burden of brevity falls on you and not your readers. Take the time to distil your thinking down to its most concentrated form.

I'm a commuter, I fly from Jo'burg to Cape Town and back again every week. A while back I decided that this book should be written on my weekly commute *(all of a sudden the flights no longer seemed like a chore - every commuter should try it)*, and only on that flight. Not a word has been written while on terra firma. The flight lasts two hours and my challenge was that if I was going to write the book on a series of two hour flights, you were going to be able to read it on one.

That's my gift to you, a bunch of my thoughts distilled into a two hour flight of ideas. Truth be told though, it's my hope that you spend a lot more than two hours thinking of the concepts I've introduced. I hope that you put this book down, and start asking **"Why do we do that?"** a whole lot more.

Remember: It's impossible to launch into tomorrow if you're anchored into yesterday.

Passenger Richard Mulholland
Seat 1c
Kulula Airlines flight MN464 from Cape Town to Lanseria
13th September 2014